# NO
# MATTER
# WHAT

# NO MATTER WHAT

## A STORY OF UNWAVERING DEVOTION
## AND THE POWER OF RESILIENCE

# ERIN NICHOLS

REDCLIFF

PUBLISHING

Published and distributed by Redcliff Publishing
Redding, CA
www.redcliffpub.com

Library of Congress Control Number: 2023921186

*Erin Nichols*
*No Matter What*

ISBN 978-1-7367095-5-9 Paperback
ISBN 978-1-7367095-6-6 eBook
ISBN 978-1-7367095-7-3 Hardcover

# DEDICATION

For Sam—my best friend, my love, my hero
and for our Kilo 3/12 brothers.

Frater Infinitas.

# CONTENTS

# PREFACE

You are about to read a collection of stories about my time with my husband—my late husband, Sam. We lived an extraordinary life together, not because of particularly ambitious undertakings on our part, but simply by the way we chose to live amidst incredibly challenging and painful circumstances.

I only know our relationship from the inside, but I've been told many times that we had something special. From our early years as teenagers in love to a young married couple finding our way after Sam's life-changing injury, others yearned for a love like ours.

I believe what set us apart stemmed from a promise we made to each other before we exchanged wedding vows on the shores of Folsom Lake in California. We were just eighteen when Sam looked at me intently and said, "Promise me we'll never let ourselves go." What he meant by that statement and the significance of the promise that followed is that we would never stop trying—in whatever we faced in life. We wouldn't allow each other to become complacent, to just exist in an endless Groundhog's Day where the only change was our waistlines. We promised each other to live each day to its fullest—to never give up on each other, on ourselves, or what was possible.

When we made that promise, we had no idea to what level it would be tested. We were handed an unfortunate set of circumstances that couldn't be changed or controlled. We could, however, choose our attitude, be intentional in the perspective we took, and be mindful of the way we chose to approach each day—even if that day would be spent in the ICU, not knowing how many more days would follow.

As you read our story, I hope you will see it could be your story too. I don't mean the same events and experiences—your life's challenges will look different than Sam's and mine. But whatever your experiences, I hope you can use the mindset we did—that no matter the challenge, you can find goodness in every moment. Time spent dwelling on the negative is time and energy you will never get back. Time spent making the most of your circumstances creates memories that inspire stories of hope and courage—the way I think of Sam's and my story.

Many people believe they are stuck with their lot in life, but we have the agency to persist, resist, and evolve. The question is, when survival is the name of the game, will you merely endure your circumstances, or will you find a way to thrive no matter what?

# CHAPTER ONE

# OUR FIRST INTRODUCTION

Formerly orange groves, and before that cattle lands and home to the Maidu Indians, my high school in Orangevale, CA, is where this part of my story begins. Casa Roble High School sits along the rolling hills of an idyllic landscape of ancient oak groves and horse properties in the Sacramento Valley. Casa Roble was my high school of choice, but in order to attend, I had to commit to two years in Junior Reserve Officers' Training Corps (ROTC).

One blazing hot August day a couple of weeks before the start of the 1997-1998 school year, I reported for the first day of Casa Roble Summer Leadership, a kind of basic training for incoming ROTC freshmen and a leadership opportunity for the older cadets. Seeking a reprieve from the unrelenting heat, I was standing alone under the tree in front of the ROTC room when a tall, ridiculously cute James Dean-looking freshman sauntered my way. I may have even looked behind me to see where he was headed because up until this point, no cute boy had ever paid me any attention as anything other than a friend.

Sure enough, I was his target. He confidently shook my hand and introduced himself as Sam, topping it off with a suave kiss on the cheek. My knees buckled. I don't know how I didn't hit the ground. What was this cute boy doing talking to me? *And* a peck on the cheek? Who's life was this?

Looking back now as a thirty-eight-year-old, it's hilarious to think this move worked on me. It certainly wouldn't work today… I don't think. If a strange, albeit good-looking, man kissed me on the cheek as he introduced himself, I'd have my defenses way up. He'd have to have some kind of charm to keep me from slapping him. But Sam had that charm. And those blue eyes.

Maybe fourteen-year-old Erin would have recoiled in horror had it been anyone other than Sam. I'm sure I wasn't the only girl he'd graced with such an introduction. I would soon learn that Sam was known as a bit of a Casanova (even at fourteen), so maybe being singled out as an object of his affection stroked my naive little ego in a way it craved.

Could this go somewhere?

## FIRST DATE

"Going somewhere" took a while. Almost a year later, the day before our first official date, Sam called me on my mom's cell phone, a behemoth of a Motorola flip phone complete with a leather case and an extending antenna. "Hey, Erin, Jake and I are going miniature golfing. Want to come?"

"Uh… you mean today?"

"Yeah, like in an hour."

"Uh, well… so Jake's going, too?"

"Sure. C'mon, you want to go with us?"

"Well… yeah… I guess. Uh… okay. Cool!"

When I hung up, my feet barely touched the ground. I was so elated to see Sam a day early.

Where Sam made me nervous, I was comfortable with Jake, the perfect man to ease my nerves. He was in my class, and we'd been friends since the beginning of freshman year, almost a year now. But Sam and Jake knew each other from middle school when Sam was in seventh grade and Jake in eighth, so they were at ease with each other. I felt electric being with Sam, so Jake proved a calming and grounding presence for me. I really don't remember much about the miniature golfing portion on the Jake-chaperoned pre-date, but what I do remember was going to Sunrise Mall across the street afterward. We wandered around, stopping at Suncoast Video and Coach House Gifts, where you could buy anything from Beanie Babies to a miniature Zen garden to hermit crabs. At some point, walking through the mall, everything became a blur. I felt warm and tingly and not quite in control of my body. Sam was holding my hand!

It turns out we would always be hand holders, and it all started with butterflies in the Sunrise Mall and the smell of Auntie Anne's Pretzels in the air. After Sam was injured, he always had to be touching me in some way. He would often put my hand to his mouth and kiss it, which a photographer even caught in a candid moment during a family photo shoot. Hand in hand, we made our way to Baskin Robbins, where Sam suggested we share a mocha blast—some sort of coffee-flavored milkshake creation. I hated coffee back then, but I loved the idea of sharing a drink with him. So, instead of suggesting something I liked (hello mint chip), I went with it, just thrilled to share a straw with him. Years later, Sam revealed that he went with the coffee flavor to seem more grown-up. Cute. So Sam.

The rest of that pre-date is a blur. I was ready for the real thing. And as much as I loved Jake, Sam and I were on firm footing, and it was time to dump the third wheel.

The next day, our moms dropped us off at the very same miniature golf and fun center as the day before, but this time, it was just the two of us. This fun center was not the big, popular one in our area, but a tiny, ramshackle place situated on a little-traveled side street in the middle of the shopping district of our small city. We may have been the only customers there at the time... or maybe it just felt that way.

As much as I didn't want Jake there, I was incredibly nervous to be alone with Sam—I couldn't believe it was actually happening. This was my first date. He was "experienced." I was only fifteen, but I had always been a tomboy—still was. Heck, I still am. Boys had always been my buddies, never seeing me as anything but one of the guys. To them, it was cool that a girl could bunny hop a bike, throw a perfect spiral, and nail jump shots. I never thought I'd draw the attention of a cute guy, especially when there were so many other girls. Prettier girls. Cooler girls. Girlier girls. But there we were.

When we finished playing, we claimed the empty, fenced-off picnic area reserved for parties. Nobody wanted to see what came next anyway. I'm a little mortified to tell you about it now.

We sat side by side at a splintery old picnic table. If the activities had done anything to quell my nerves, they were back in full force now. To this day, I've never experienced such intense butterflies. Our knees touching, we shared some awkward conversation. Sam admitted that he'd had a crush on me since the beginning of the last school year. I demurely admitted the same. This was getting serious. Were my palms always this wet? Where was Jake now?

After more awkward conversation, Sam suggested we go to Jimboy's Tacos (a Sacramento institution) across the street. I agreed (of course I did, I couldn't think straight enough to have an opinion). But before I could get up, Sam stopped me and said, "So… can I kiss you now?"

Holy crap! It was really happening!

I mumbled something to the affirmative, and so began an epic make-out session. Yeah…we were those teenagers. My body had never experienced so much tension, yet it was melting. I kept realizing I was squeezing him too tight and would force myself to relax, only to tighten back up again a moment later.

Multiple times, he suggested we head over to Jimboy's, but before either of us could initiate getting up, we were drawn together yet again. Eventually, our lips were getting raw. And even though he was only fourteen, Sam already had a scratchy five o'clock shadow that was tearing up my face. So, we reluctantly unclenched and set out hand-in-hand to refuel with greasy tacos.

On our way over, Sam mentioned that he loved how tightly I held onto him. What had been making me feel self-conscious now made me feel special. It wasn't the last time, either. Sam would keep finding ways to make me feel that way.

## YOUNG LOVE

When the school year began a few weeks later, Sam was a sophomore, and I was a junior. We had been dating for a couple of months and were feeling like the unofficial ROTC super couple, but at this point in our relationship, we had not deemed ourselves boyfriend and girlfriend. I wasn't sure why, and my insecurity could hardly handle the uncertainty. But I didn't have the confidence in myself or where I stood with Sam to bring it up myself, so I waited for him to make the move.

On the morning of the 1999 Titan ROTC Drill Competition at Fairfield High School, my mom drove us and three other kids to the event. Sam was the commander of several armed teams, meaning they used either sabers, rifles, or replica rifles to perform choreographed, precise, and uniform marching movements. I commanded the unarmed exhibition team and performed on two or three other teams. But before it all, Sam and I had a private moment in an empty hallway. Butterflies flitted in my stomach as he held both my hands, looked into my eyes, and said, "I could easily fall in love with you." Whew! He sure was good at buckling my knees. How could this be happening to me? I was *so* into him it was hard to believe. And apparently, he felt the same. We snuck in a quick but meaningful kiss and returned to our teams.

We crushed the competition. Endorphins pumping through our pubescent bodies after winning the sweepstakes trophy at the drill competition, Sam and I sat with my mom and a few friends at a table at Leatherby's, our local ice cream shop. As the revelry waned and empty ice cream dishes and smudges of hot fudge littered the blue and white marbled table, a couple of kids got up to use the restroom. Sam pulled his ever-present pen from his pocket and grabbed a napkin from the chrome dispenser. Covering his work like a third grader during a spelling test, he wrote and then slid the napkin over to me. "So, do you wanna make us official?"

"Very much," I replied and slid the napkin back.

"So, now?"

"Yes."

Sam and Erin, or Sam and "Nernie" (my nickname from childhood, which would forever be Sam's pet name for me), were officially boyfriend and girlfriend.

That napkin sits framed on a bookshelf in my living room. And it wouldn't be the only time he used a napkin to romance me.

We became best friends, wanting to do nothing more than be with each other or talk on the phone. Most of our dates involved watching a movie at my house or his. Sam was a big film buff, so he delighted in exposing me to the great movies of the 80s and 90s that I'd missed. The first one he ever brought to my house was *Pulp Fiction*.

We were still only fifteen years old, and I can see how difficult it is for many to wrap their minds around two young teenagers actually being in love. As much as it was possible at our age and maturity, we were falling—like a '60s heroine slipping into quicksand—in love. But I didn't want to be rescued.

Exactly a week after we'd become "official," Sam and a couple of friends were hanging out at my house when my mom suggested we go up to Apple Hill, a region in the Sierra Nevada foothills full of apple orchards and apple products: fresh apple pie, cider, apple donuts—if you can make it from an apple, they have it. We were going on an impromptu road trip for pie. Sweet!

Sam cocked his head to the side, made a goofy grin, and with childish glee declared, "I like pie!" About an hour and a half into the journey, my mom pulled over at a breathtaking overlook of Donner Lake. As if a giant ice cream scoop had carved out a great valley from the land, green mountains topped with snow surrounded a swath of dark blue below us. Something wasn't right, though.

Did we go the right way? We had just passed Donner Summit at over 7,000 feet elevation, and the Nevada border was getting closer and closer. My mom called my grandma to check her directions. Yep, we were on the wrong freeway and were eighty-five miles into the heart of the Sierra Nevada mountain range.

So we turned around and headed back down the mountain for another hour, only to land at Marie Callender's, just three miles from home. By now, we were all starving, but we were determined to finally get our pie.

As we waited for a table, Sam and Brendan went to Longs Drugs on a secret mission. Sam's goofy grin was back as he hid something behind him and sat down next to me. He was all smiles when he coyly presented me with a little white teddy bear, its arms and legs stuck out to the sides as if awaiting a hug. Between them was a folded napkin that I unfolded to see, "Happy Week-aversary! I like you thiiiiiiis much."

Oh, man! This guy! How did I deserve such a thoughtful boyfriend? Pie never tasted so good or had been worth such a long wait.

A couple of weeks later, an ROTC friend was temporarily staying at my house when Sam came over. Wanting some privacy from her and my little sister, Sam and I escaped to my mom's new van in the garage—a hunter-green Toyota Sienna which boasted sixteen cupholders and a strong new-car smell. When we turned the leather captain's chairs toward each other, he held both my hands. "I have something to tell you." Poof! The garage lights went off. We heard girlish giggles inside the house. There we sat in near-complete darkness when he said, "I love you."

"I love you too."

And so began our first make-out session as a couple in love.

CHAPTER TWO

# OUR EARLY RELATIONSHIP

Sam and I soon became the couple everyone wanted to be. In all honesty, though, I don't get what Sam saw in me then. I'm a catch now, but I was awkward as hell back then, rarely wore makeup, and dressed like a P.E. teacher with body dysmorphia. (Now I dress like a P.E. teacher who's proud of her curves and muscles.)

Sam was the desirable one. Guys wanted to be like him (handsome, charming, intelligent, with a dry wit), and girls wanted to be with him. Though there was a mile-long list of girls who wanted Sam, I can't say there was the same level of interest in me from guys. So, other than believing in true love and finding your person (or lobster if you're a *Friends* fan), I don't know how to explain his attraction and adoring love for me. Even though he never did anything to make me feel insecure (he did the opposite, in fact, showering me with praise and affection), I always felt like he had the upper hand in our relationship. We spent our time before and after school and at lunch in our home base on

13

campus, the ROTC room. Whenever logistically possible, Sam walked me to my classes, leaving me at the door with a kiss. One semester, we had 4th period across the hall from each other, which gave us more time to canoodle in the hallway. Either Frau Mac, his German teacher, or Ms. Cooper, my English teacher, frequently busted us for PDA (public display of affection), dragging us apart and into our respective classrooms.

Getting my license at the end of my junior year was a game-changer for my independence and our time together. Now, instead of my mom or Sam's brother driving us, we had all that commute time to ourselves to talk, joke, and make plans as we drove and then canoodled in the parking lot before tearing ourselves apart to get to class. In my senior year, his junior year, I drove him to and from school in my white 1996 Honda Civic. Wednesdays were trash pickup days in his neighborhood. As I drove down his street, I'd pretend to swerve toward the trash cans along the roadside, making explosion sound effects as I went. No matter how often I did it, Sam always played along and cracked up. In the compact confines of the Civic, I tended to drive left-handed, with my right hand on Sam's thigh, always needing to be in contact with him. When he got his license, Sam confessed he'd practiced driving his mom's automatic Chevy Malibu with his right hand on the gear shift to reciprocate my tender practice.

We typically spent a few afternoons a week after school together, depending on our school workloads, usually picking up something to eat at Jack in the Box or getting KFC's Honey BBQ wings, a favorite of Sam's. In the evening, we watched movies, played video games, and surreptitiously took advantage of his bedroom being at the far end of the hallway. Ahem.

When Sam and I were sixteen and seventeen, we, along with his brother, Donny, got hired as server assistants at Northridge Country

Club in Fair Oaks. We had our fair share of clandestine moments in the supply room, but having grown up in his dad's restaurants, Sam hated food service. So he only worked at the country club for about two months before moving on to Albertson's supermarket. Our lives, while separate, were quite entangled for a couple of teenagers. This spoke to our closeness and friendship but also led to some rocky times.

## I CAN'T DO THIS ANYMORE

Sam had made me feel seen in a way I'd never experienced before. He made me feel sexy, which isn't an adjective I'd ever used to describe myself. Our intelligence, humor, and homebody nature made us a good pair. Though we enjoyed music, playing games—mostly video games, all things martial arts—and watching movies, most of all, we loved talking together. We had that spark.

We rarely fought, but when we did, it was related to boundaries, or my lack thereof, and his lies to attempt to spare my feelings. Because we felt like we were forever and even talked about it, I tended to expect our relationship to operate more like a marriage than a young love between a couple of teenagers.

He had parents and family obligations outside of me, and my fragile, insecure ego felt slighted whenever I wasn't invited to his family affairs. Or when he wanted to spend time with his brothers or friends instead of me. In contrast, my family welcomed Sam to any family event. If he wasn't there, they'd ask where he was. We were a package deal, and where I was, he was expected. It's not that his family didn't welcome and accept me, because they did. But sometimes, he just needed to be Sam, not "SamnErin." This wasn't something I understood until later, though.

So he would try to spare my feelings (or just not deal with them) by lying about where he was or what he had to do. Every time, his wanting to spend time with anyone other than me felt like rejection, a deep fear of mine that would come back to bite me.

One mid-June afternoon, with the oppressive heat of summer in the Sacramento Valley upon us, Sam called and asked if he could come over. He had just completed his junior year of high school and had his license. I had just graduated. My excitement of him randomly asking to come over vanished as I saw the seriousness on his face at the door. Standing in the entryway, with no other explanation, he confessed, "I can't do this anymore."

The "this" he couldn't do anymore was us. I was completely blind-sided, in utter disbelief. I felt like my heart had been ripped out and that we were both standing there, looking at it sputtering on the floor between us. When I probed further, unable to process what was happening, all he could tell me was that we were too serious. I needed too much from him. He needed time just to be Sam. The truly crushing part was that I knew he was right.

But at least he hadn't cheated. This was my biggest fear. He assured me there was no one else. It's telling that this was my first thought, but my insecurities about his good looks and charm always made me wary of the influence and beauty of other girls. I always feared eventually, he'd find a girl that matched his good looks.

In retrospect, there were indicators that things weren't going great. He'd been distant. He didn't come to my high school graduation, claiming the traffic was too bad leading up to the school. I had to convince him to meet us at Leatherby's (home of making us "official") after, to celebrate. I'd felt my too-tight grasp on him slipping but was in denial. It couldn't be, I told myself. We were "SamnErin." We were supposed to be together forever. Surely, if I just held on tighter…But then he left, and I was broken and confused. My first love—gone. I truly felt he was my one and only love. Waves of disbelief and grief washed over me. Somehow, I made it through my shift at the country club that night. I probably should have called in sick, but I didn't want to be the type of girl who let a breakup ruin her life. Even though I *was* that type of girl, I didn't want to *seem* like that type of girl.

My boss, Mary, had known Sam since he was a little boy, having worked for his dad at Coco's Diner many years before. So I let her in on my red-rimmed, puffy eyes, and she did her best to comfort me and take it easy on me. She knew how special Sam and I were together. Serving and clearing food for the local 1%, I couldn't stop questioning myself and my reality. Was this really happening? What did I do wrong? Surely, this wasn't forever.

With time, I eventually came to realize our true problem: He was my first boyfriend. But I was not his first girlfriend. I had fallen madly in love at fifteen years old with no experience and lacked the emotional maturity not to screw it up. My feelings were far too strong to deal with them rationally. Neither of us had the capacity, as hormonal teenagers, to deal well with the overwhelmingly emotional state of being in love.

We were sixteen and seventeen, but I acted like we were married. I was needy and clingy. My insecurity that he would leave caused me to hold on too tight. I couldn't let him or the relationship breathe. We were "SamnErin," and I had no concept of Erin outside our codependent relationship. He just wanted to be Sam. My own sense of self was so ill-formed at the time that I thought I needed him. I would eventually learn that I didn't *need* him, but I *wanted* him.

## WHO HURT ME?

Why was I so insecure? Why was I so needy? Why did I hold on too tight?

It wasn't my parents. I had the most loving and supportive parents a kid could ask for. I wasn't bullied. I didn't grow up in the age of social media. There's only one tiny event I can remember that shaped this part of my personality.

Citrus Heights, where I grew up, is a suburb of Sacramento. We lived on a cul-de-sac with sixteen houses and thirty kids, and I was never short of friends to play with… almost.

One day, when I was four years old, my friend and neighbor, Brigette, one year older than me, was over playing. Someone knocked at the door—our neighbor, four-year-old Monica. She came looking for Brigette, and the two of them left together, leaving me shattered, confused, and alone.

Watching them walk away, chatting and laughing, made me feel that I wasn't good enough, not worth spending time with. My young, impressionable brain learned that they had something I didn't, and there will always be someone better than me.

My heart breaks for that little-girl Erin—that she experienced this rejection and suffered the profound impact it had on who I would later become.

Then again…we're all the sum of our experiences, and I'm pretty happy with who I am today. Maybe it took four-year-old Erin getting ditched to make me into the person I am today. Maybe that was my first real experience of resilience—a trait I would come to be known for.

## I CAN'T DO THIS ANYMORE

Briefly, during the five months Sam and I were broken up, we dated other people and each other. I don't remember how it started, but he must have called to ask me out. I do remember wearing a skirt, which I never wear or wore, on our second "first" date at Scandia—a miniature golf and fun center with a batting cage, bumper cars, and an arcade. I guess I wanted to drive him a little crazy. I guess it worked because midway through our round, we were kissing and holding hands.

I was still a virgin and would remain so until after we got back together for good, but there was a fair bit of fooling around. Those evenings always ended painfully for me. I loved being with Sam. I loved him, but he apparently didn't feel the same way, or at least wasn't ready for it to be forever. Who could blame him? He was just turning seventeen.

Since we weren't actually together, none of the issues that led to our breakup could be worked on. After about a month of this, I told him *I* couldn't do it anymore. I couldn't do this halfway thing. It hurt too bad. Either we were together, and we worked on our issues—mainly communication and boundaries—or we didn't see each other anymore. That's probably one of my proudest moments. I loved him *so* much, but I loved me more. Even if it meant losing him forever, I couldn't keep letting him hurt me.

I didn't become the girl who let a breakup ruin her life, but life has a way of circling back around when we least expect it.

There he was, tall, smiling, and perfect. Everything stopped. My heart was in my throat. My eyes stung with squelched tears. All sounds ceased. All I could see was Sam standing there in front of me in the middle of the mall. I hadn't seen him in months. We shared an awkward hug. I didn't want to let go, but he wasn't mine to hold onto.

We must have shared some pleasantries, but all I can remember is the feeling of wanting to escape. I either needed him to hold me and never let go, or I had to walk away with my head held high without letting on that my heart was breaking.

I managed to avoid falling apart in front of him and surreptitiously slinked into a changing room in American Eagle, where I was safe to crumble, sob, and grieve. Then, I reassembled myself into some modicum of a functioning human before emerging puffy-eyed and runny-nosed.

He called me a few days later. We had an amazing, vintage "SamnErin" conversation. We talked for over an hour, and it felt just like the old days but also somehow different. Even though our chemistry was still there, I felt more in control of myself—my feelings.

I changed and had grown over the past several months. I existed without him. I wasn't happy about it but I still did it. I didn't need him in the same codependent, desperate way I needed him before. Instead, I just felt really good talking to him and felt more like my true self than I ever had. He suggested that we hang out soon. I was attending a local community college, and he was a senior in high school, so I offered to pick him up from school later in the week when I had an early day. It was a date.

On November 7, 2001, I arrived at our high school with my stomach in knots. Were we going to be friends? Could we be just friends? I couldn't allow myself to hope for more, but in my heart of hearts, I knew we were supposed to be together—or at least that my heart couldn't bear any other possibility.

I headed from the student parking lot toward the ROTC room, where I expected he'd be. This was before texting, and he only had a pager, so I would have to actually track him down. *There he was!* We saw each other and smiled. The music surged, the rotation of the Earth slowed, and all but the two of us dissolved into a haze. We walked toward each other, eyes locked.

"Erin! Hey Erin! What are you doing here?!" called our mutual friend, Jessica, completely ruining our romantic comedy reunification scene.

The magic of the moment was over, but Sam and I saw the humor in it. We went to the ROTC room so I could see some old friends, very aware that all eyes were on us. Faces questioning whether we were back together.

Driving us to his house in the trusty Civic, I stopped myself from the default of resting my right hand on his left thigh. In his room, we watched a movie on his red velvet-covered futon with a Pee Wee Herman doll hanging over it and the Scooby Doo stuffed animal I'd bought him for his birthday on top of his twenty-inch Toshiba TV. But later, neither of us could ever remember what the movie was. We started the movie sitting near each other on the futon, but somehow, by the end of the movie, I was snuggled up under his left arm, my head on his shoulder. The credits rolled. He looked down and asked me a question about the movie. I looked up at him to answer, our faces only inches apart, and we kissed.

It was warm, dry clothes on a rainy day, ice-cold lemonade in the sweltering heat, slipping into an old favorite pair of jeans, or taking off your bra at the end of a long day. We were home. We were where we belonged. We were back together... forever.

After we got back together, Sam told me I had broken his heart. I won't lie and say that it didn't feel good. Knowing I had as much influence over his heart as he did mine was gratifying— but not in a revengeful kind of way. It just felt good to know that he loved me enough to be heartbroken.

A week or so later—before we told anyone we were back together again—Sam called while my sister was hanging out in my room with me. All my family knew was that we had hung out a few times. As we ended the phone call, my sister heard me say, "You too."

"He said I love you! You guys are back together!"

"Yeah, but please don't tell anyone."

It still felt too good to be true, and I didn't want to jinx it. I was afraid that once I announced it to my family, he would change his mind and dump me again. As secure as I felt when we were together, my insecurity in his devotion to me would take a while to heal. Eventually, and especially after his injury, his devotion and love for me would be the most sure I felt of anything in this world.

We felt right together. But it also felt like keeping it a secret protected me from anything going wrong. I felt safe in our little bubble.

A few weeks later was my eighteenth and my sister's fourteenth birthdays, one day apart. My family was getting together at TGI Fridays to celebrate, and I invited Sam. We never announced we were back together, but we didn't hide our affection, and what everyone thought to be inevitable came to fruition. I saw that our families picked up on the spark between us, the once-in-a-lifetime love. They clearly expected us to be together for good.

Sam and I quickly fell into a rhythm. I attended Sierra College, a community college in nearby Rocklin, CA, while he finished up his senior year of high school at Casa Roble. I spent most evenings hanging out at his house, and by the end of his senior year (2002) we were talking about getting our own apartment.

His dad, however, saw the folly in this plan. We both worked part time. As much as we thought it would be feasible, he knew we'd have to work full time to make it on our own, which would mean no time for school.

I was already underachieving in the eyes of many. I could have taken the ROTC scholarship and had a full ride to any university with a Senior ROTC program. I had a 3.9 GPA, was the top cadet of my unit, and had won Cadet of the Semester, a regional award.

When I made the decision to attend community college instead of applying to universities and pursuing the scholarship, I was madly in love with my high school boyfriend. I'd briefly entertained the idea of joining the U.S. Air Force—my grandpa and uncle were career Air Force men, and my dad served five years. If I hadn't been with Sam, that's probably the way I would have gone. But other than Sam, I didn't know what I wanted. I was scared to leave home, scared to make a life-changing decision, and scared to grow up.

Sam's parents offered me their oldest son's old bedroom with the expectation that I would sleep in my own room. Done deal! I moved in as soon as Sam graduated. Our parents didn't want us to have to work so much that we couldn't still go to college. Sam didn't know what he wanted to do either, but his parents knew that working full-time to support ourselves instead of going to school wasn't going to help us figure it out.

# CHAPTER THREE

# LOST PHILOSOPHERS

The next school year, Sam and I were in different philosophy classes at our community college. We spent a good deal of time in those days waxing poetic about success and the future and what we discussed in philosophy class.

Sam was feeling particularly verbose when, years later, I asked him about this period of our lives. "We were not but a couple of teens with lofty ideals and high hopes for the future and no idea how to achieve any of it. We didn't even know what our goals were to attempt to achieve them. We were so overwhelmed by the sheer enormity of possibilities we were crippled to move forward. We were each considered intelligent kids with high potential, but this only added to the pressure of making something of ourselves." I concur.

Riding home in my Civic, we often talked about how great it would be just to drive off and leave, landing in some faraway place from home and starting our lives. We'd get jobs and an apartment and live happily ever after. We were young and naive, and all we really knew was that wherever we ended up, it would be together.

Sam worked part time as a bag boy at Albertson's supermarket, and I sold cars at CarMax. We lived at his parents' house, in separate bedrooms, and although we were only eighteen and nineteen, we were often asked when we would get married. Everyone saw our love and devotion as undeniable. We knew it would happen one day, but we felt overwhelmed at the prospect of being out on our own.

Neither of us knew what we wanted to be when we grew up—in my case, the answer changed monthly. My aspirations ranged from an EMT to a physical therapist, an anthropologist to an English teacher. All we knew for sure was that we wanted to be together. As things stood, if we got married, we'd still be working part-time, going to community college, and living at his parents' house. The only practical difference would be that we'd share a room at night.

I had just come home from a long day of work at CarMax when Sam called me into his room. He wanted to talk. My heart started racing. I had never seen him so nervous. My stomach was in my throat. Was he breaking up with me—again? Sensing my anxiety, he assured me that he loved me and everything was okay. We sat on the edge of the bed as he divulged his desire—no, his need—to enlist in the military.

Reflecting back on this day many years later, Sam said, "I decided I wanted to join the Marine Corps because I wanted to get out of my house and grow up and become a man." This would fulfill his natural sense of chivalry, service, and honor. I always said he was born in the wrong century.

Believe it or not, I was relieved. I come from a military family. The notion of living on base and having a secure paycheck with medical and housing was more than I could have dreamed of at that age. Enlistment solved all our problems. He was shocked at my excitement. "This means we can get married!" I declared. It wasn't so much a proposal as a logistical decision. We were always planning on getting married— enlisting just enabled us to do it sooner.

Sam had a slightly different perspective: "I didn't know what we should do, but when Erin suggested getting married right away, I thought we needed to wait until after boot camp. Unbeknownst to Erin, I felt it was too soon for both of us, but I decided we should go ahead and get married. Just being together and in love, while knowing the future was secure eased my mind."

Our friend, Josh, had just signed with the Marines a couple of months before. He had another month or two before he left for boot camp, so we figured Sam would have four to six months before he would leave. That meant we needed to get married that summer in order to ensure our wedding was on our terms rather than on the Marine Corps'.

With my mom's help, we shopped for a ring at a local jewelry store not too far from our house. The one I picked out had to be ordered. Apparently, the jewelry industry slows down around Passover, so the ring—and Sam's official proposal— took longer than expected to arrive. I'll never forget, I was sitting at CarMax's customer-facing window when Sam showed up with his brother, holding a Jamba Juice for me. I was thrilled! I looked around at the other girls in the business office, making sure they knew what a handsome catch I had. *Ladies, this is the kind of man you're looking for!* And he'd surprised me with a *Strawberries Wild!*

When I turned back to face Sam, framed by the gray of the business office window, he was holding out the engagement ring. "You gotta marry me."

I was stunned. I knew it was going to happen, but I couldn't believe it. I was still elated about my Jamba Juice, but now the diamond, so sparkly in the corporate overhead lighting, took my breath away. "Hang on," I said, stripping the till drawer key off my arm and handing it to my co-worker.

Shaking and in shock, I stepped into the hallway where Sam stood, grabbed his hand, and pulled him outside. There, surrounded by the blue and yellow CarMax colors, Sam dropped to a knee, held up the ring, and ever so romantically said, "Marry the shit out of me."

## WEDDING DAY

Given our short timeline, the wedding needed to be planned in a hurry. We wanted a simple ceremony, but one like we'd never attended. For us, the day was not about extravagance or a huge party—it was the first day of our marriage.

If it weren't for the deep respect we both had for our parents, we would have gotten married at city hall. But since we decided to have a wedding for our family, it was going to be our style—casual. Our wedding invitation, created on my computer, was in the style of a flier for a neighborhood barbecue. On it, we announced that ties would be confiscated and that guests should bring their swimming gear for a dip in the lake after the ceremony. It was 105°F that day—July 27, 2003, so a fair number of guests took us up on the offer. Almost any July day in Folsom, California, is assaulted with extreme heat—but hey, it's a dry heat—so we scheduled our wedding for 11:00 a.m.

We rented the little community center at Folsom Lake. Folsom, as in Johnny Cash: Live at Folsom Prison. It was local and inexpensive, and we both grew up going there. In the middle of the summer heat, the community center provided a welcoming air-conditioned space with a kitchen and bathrooms. Plus, it had a nice outdoor deck for dancing, if that's your thing.

Outside, we had ample room to set up chairs theater-style on a gentle slope under the trees, looking out at the lake with the foothills rising in the distance. We chose an island theme, and from the pictures, it was so realistic it fools everyone who wasn't there in person.

I have a vague memory of sitting in the back seat of someone else's car, but I really don't remember arriving at the lake. What I do clearly remember is being in the kitchen with my cousin and bridesmaid, Tricia, peeking out the door to see Sam standing outside with his groomsmen—his two older brothers and my cousin, Ira.

That's when I had a minor anxiety attack. Back then, I rarely noticed my anxiety until my hands were already tingling. Looking out the door at Sam, I was tingly alright. It wasn't a fear of getting married or questioning whether or not we were doing the right thing. It was nervousness about the ceremony and all eyes being on us during a very personal and intimate moment of our lives.

I was simply more excited about being married than I had been about anything else in my life.

As part of our Hawaiian-themed wedding and a nod to Sam's love of Japan and martial arts, we created an aisle using bamboo Goza mats, splitting the two sections of folding, white rental chairs nestled in a clearing of forest overlooking Folsom Lake. It gave somewhat of an indoor effect to our outdoor wedding but had the drawback of being quite slippery. The combination of bamboo mats and the foam soles of my flip-flops left me quite unsteady as I traversed the gentle slope toward my groom. I'm sure there's a metaphor there.

Later, I asked Sam about how he was feeling as the ceremony started. "Everything with us was wonderful. When I saw Erin walking down the aisle, I thought, 'That is the one girl I can spend all my days with.'"

My mom and dad both walked me down the aisle, one on either side, because of my unsure footing. They were literally helping hold me up (more metaphor) by gripping an elbow on one side and my upper arm on the other. But it looked like they were dragging me down the aisle. It wasn't a shotgun wedding; it just looked like one.

I survived the treacherous journey and was rewarded by my husband-to-be beaming at me with his big, warm smile and his amazing blue eyes. I couldn't believe this was it. It was really happening! With all the stress of the planning and logistics of the wedding, this was what I had been sick with anticipation for, standing there looking at this man who was about to devote his life to me as I was devoting mine to him. "Hold on," I said. "There's just a…" I reached up and plucked a bit of fuzz from Sam's goatee. Our guests laughed and "awwwed" over my literal nit-picking.

Despite the 150-200 of our closest friends and family looking on, I had no awareness of their presence once the ceremony started. My only distraction from the power of the moment was the sweat dripping between my boobs as the midday sun blasted down on us.

Sam and I decided we wouldn't kiss the week before the wedding, which turned out to be far more difficult than we thought—not so much out of desire but more due to our well-established habit. More than once, one of us had to quickly turn our cheek to thwart the other's incoming kiss. Now that we were on the precipice of our first kiss as husband and wife, however, desire was at the forefront—and he really did have perfect lips.

We said our vows. I, for some reason, couldn't help but giggle the whole way through mine. Sam, of course, was perfectly sincere, his blue eyes staring unrelentingly into mine. Finally, our minister—Morey, a family friend I've known since I was six, was about to wrap it up. At last, the kiss was coming. But instead of "You may now kiss the bride," Morey introduced the Lord's Supper. Doh! We forgot we had decided to take communion. As the realization of our delayed kiss settled on each of us, we lowered our heads, foreheads touching, in what hopefully appeared to be reverence–but was definitely disappointment.

The extended anticipation made our first kiss as husband and wife all that more special. Sam was officially and legally mine. We spent the next several hours with our closest family and friends, celebrating our newly-wedded bliss at our reception, kicked off by our Australian DJ, Terry.

Terry set up on the sweltering outdoor deck of the community center. He played Bob Marley's "Is This Love" for our wedding song. It was too hot to dance, and I don't like dancing anyway, but we still followed tradition and participated in a few obligatory wedding dances. Once they were over, I was happy to hang out and talk to our guests with Terry's music creating the ambiance. In high school, Sam and I were on the Military Ball Committee for our Junior ROTC formal, and Terry was the DJ for the event. Sam and I had taken on many of the organizing tasks together, including choosing the song on which the ball's theme would be based. Sam was very into music and definitely a romantic. As we brainstormed in the ROTC staff room (a kind of non-secret lair for the cadets on staff and our home base), Sam looked at me with his teal-blue eyes, grabbed both of my hands and in his best Al Green tenor, started singing,"I-I-I, mmm babe, I'm sooo in love with you…" Alright! Song chosen! Damn, Sam was smooth. I made sure Terry had that song at the top of his list.

It just seemed natural that we would hire Terry two years later to DJ at our island-themed wedding reception. As the festivities were winding down, Terry announced the last song of the day and Al Green's smooth voice declared, "I'm so in love with you." Our song! We hadn't asked Terry to play it. We hadn't even told him it had become our song, but somehow, he remembered it from the Junior ROTC formal. I looked across the room to my husband, and our eyes met. Sam led me out to the deck in front of Terry and all our friends and family to dance to "Let's Stay Together."Marriage was forever for both of us. After Sam got hurt, I never once considered leaving him. In fact, it floored me whenever someone suggested that or said they admired me for staying with him. I was his world, and he was mine. "Let's Stay Together" went from being our song to our anthem. Even after his injury, every time we heard the song, he'd sing it to me, grabbing me with his one working hand to dance. He always had the moves. I just followed. By four in the afternoon, we had everything packed up and were checking into a local hotel in Historic Folsom. After changing clothes and counting our wedding booty, we hit up the local Chevy's Fresh Mex for dinner. Yeah, we were ballers. We'd just sat down at our table—only the finest booth for the newlyweds—when we were surprised by a high school friend, Carl, as our server. He inquired about what we'd been up to, and when Sam announced that we just got married, Carl congratulated us and asked if he could get us started with an appetizer. The food was just right, but it could have been burnt to a crisp, and I would have still loved our first meal together as a married couple.

The next morning, we started our honeymoon road trip, driving my mother-in-law's champagne-colored Chevy Malibu down to San Diego, snacking on the pizza-sized chocolate chip cookie with "Congratulations Sam and Erin" in icing she'd bought for us. Sitting in traffic on I-5 in Los Angeles, listening to Nirvana's *Nevermind* album, yet another car honked at us. What the hell?! Suddenly, it dawned on us—"Just Married" was written all over the windows. We laughed out loud just as "In Bloom" surged through the speakers. We started with two days in

San Diego, visiting the zoo and getting really sunburned on an overcast day at the beach. Next, a stay in Little Tokyo in L.A. and a trip to Universal Studios. Then, on to Long Beach for some time with Sam's brother, Donny.

From there, we planned to take the scenic Highway 1 up the coast to Monterey. I say "planned to" because after three hours, we'd only traveled about an inch on the map and still had several inches to go. Highway 1 is beautiful in spots, but it was lousy with construction, detours, and slow speed limits through quaint beach towns. I navigated as Sam drove us to the more inland route so we could arrive before our first anniversary.

Monterey was our big splurge: two nights in a classic Spanish-style inn. We put the frenzy of Southern California travel behind us and took time to slow down, to just enjoy the scenery and each other. Sam's boot camp leave date was just nine weeks away, and neither of us were ready to return to reality, so we stayed an extra night. But all good things must end. After extending our stay in Monterey, we made our way home, where we began our lives as husband and wife.

CHAPTER FOUR

# BOOT CAMP— MILITARY LIFE BEGINS

Sam's boot camp was my boot camp as well. When he stepped on the infamous yellow footprints to begin his Marine Corps career, I entered an emotional boot camp and experienced my first depression. Boot camp was twelve weeks long, and I spent them living as the only kid at my in-law's house, working my part-time job at CarMax, and sulking.

I had been in school, but with Sam's impending boot camp departure, the thought of spending any time away from him crushed me. I couldn't concentrate and had no drive to study, so I dropped all my classes a few weeks into the semester. All I wanted was to soak up as much time with him as I could before he left for twelve weeks, and our great adventure began. There'd always be time for school later.

The day I'd been dreading, yet also the day that marked an exciting new beginning in our lives, finally arrived. It was time for Sam to leave for boot camp. Although he would be trained at the Marine Corps Recruit

Depot (MCRD) in San Diego, step one was Sacramento Military Entrance Processing Station (MEPS), where he would process into the military and take his oath of enlistment. From there, he would be delivered to MCRD San Diego.

Sam's mom, dad, and I together took on the duty of delivering him to MEPS at the Radisson in Sacramento. Sam and I sat in the backseat of his mom's Chevy Malibu, holding hands like we were on a date chaperoned by his parents. He was nervous but mostly excited to become a U.S. Marine and step into the role of manhood like he always dreamed of. As I've said, Sam was born into the wrong time period. Chivalrous and brave, duty-bound and proud, Sam had the heart of a warrior, and this was his chance to fulfill a great desire of his heart. If he could have chosen, he would have been a samurai, roaming the Japanese countryside and protecting small villages from predatory bandits. Since he was born into modern-day America, the Marine Corps was the next best thing.

We arrived at the Radisson, just off the I-80 freeway, and all exited the car. Sam first embraced his parents, and they said their goodbyes. With my heart in my throat and a cannonball-sized hole in my gut, it was my turn. We held each other in a long, tight hug, my head nestled in the space between his chest and chin—my space.

"I'm so proud of you, but I don't want to let you go." I said.

"I know, but this is the first step to the life we want. I'll write as much as I can." He replied.

"I'll write every day." I promised.

"I love you so much, and I'll think of you the whole time, but I gotta go in." Sam said.

"I love you more." I argued.

40

"I love you ten times infinity and beyond." He said, delivering the who-loves-who-more trump card.

I let him go and watched my new husband take his first steps, marking the beginning of a new journey for us. This was his career, and boot camp was his experience to have, but it was my first step as well. A step into the life of a Marine wife. I should have heeded the old warning, "Watch out for that first step." Boot camp was hard on me. When I wasn't at work, I was lying on the deep purple couch at my in-laws', watching inane TV in my jammies. I could hardly care for my basic needs and didn't have the energy to cook, so I ate mostly instant mashed potatoes and canned corn. I didn't see it as depression at the time, but knowing what I know now, it was definitely situational depression. But back then, I was in denial about any mental health issues. Although I came from a family with a significant mental illness history, I wouldn't allow myself to even consider it—temporary or not—for about another ten years.

Sam and I had never gone this long without talking, even during our five-month breakup. He got one phone call on the first day of boot camp, which only lasted as long as he could rush through, "I'm here. I'm fine. I love you." Our only correspondence for twelve weeks was hand-written letters. He was able to write five or six to me, plus a couple to his parents and brothers. But I wrote to him every day, sometimes more than once. Sitting in the hand-me-down queen bed his aunt and uncle had given us, I stared at his giant Reservoir Dogs poster on the wall and a Pee Wee Herman doll hanging from the ceiling. They brought me comfort as I wrote to Sam on brightly colored paper. I shared my thoughts and feelings, random things from home or work, and expressed my love and heartache, but also my pride in him—always my pride in him. As cliché as it sounds (I hate being cliché), these letters were often dotted with tears, dimpling the paper and running the ink. To give him some comfort from home, I regularly included comic strips, hoarded away from the Sunday *Sacramento Bee*, which I parsed out one by one.

Writing these letters to Sam was the highlight of my day. It made me feel close to him, even if the conversation was one-sided. Each letter was a day closer to seeing him in person again.

## BOOT CAMP GRADUATION

When Sam's long-awaited boot camp graduation finally came, we had a good-sized entourage making the trip to San Diego. His parents, middle brother, and oldest brother's long-time girlfriend drove down and stayed in a San Diego motel. My parents, sister and I flew and were blessed to be welcomed by my lifelong friend, Meaghann, and her Marine husband, John. Their home was on base at Camp Pendleton, about forty-five minutes north of the Marine Corps Recruit Depot in San Diego, and we gratefully camped out in their living room until we could bring Sam home with us. Flying low over the city into San Diego was a trip because the plane seemed to just barely clear the city buildings. Our runway was immediately next to the MCRD obstacle course. Sam was so close I hoped against hope to spot him on the course. But, no luck. I'd have to wait another day to hug him. He'd told me how torturous it was being so painfully close to the airport that he could literally taste the fumes and how he fantasized about leaving on one of those planes or me flying in on one to surprise him.

The graduation was a two-day affair. Day one, Thursday, was family day, when the recruits would march out onto the expansive blacktop parade deck to be presented their Eagle, Globe, and Anchor (EGA), the Marine Corps emblem, with their families proudly looking on from the bleachers. Afterward, there would be a couple of hours for the newly minted Marine to hang out with his family on the MCRD grounds. Friday was the actual graduation day when we would get to take our Marine home.

I was incredibly anxious about seeing Sam. I was obviously new to being a military wife, and I'd never been to MCRD. My insecurities and fear of the unknown overtook me. I had no idea what to expect. I was the most excited and anxious I'd ever been and felt as if my insides were trying to crawl out of me. Would Sam be different? Would he still be my goofy, charming, funny Sam? Or would he have been turned into a hardened killing machine in his twelve weeks of Marine Corps boot camp? In retrospect, this fear seems almost silly. But at the time, it was real and profound. John drove us down to MCRD. Having him and Meaghann, there was an enormous source of comfort because they actually knew what was going on. John was my guide and chauffeur, getting us on base easily and directing us where we needed to be.

I can't think of another time when I was so difficult to be around, and with everything so unfamiliar and out of my control, it was not the time to ask me questions. Admittedly, I don't like not knowing the answer to a question, so being asked stuff by my family (mostly my well-meaning mom) in such uncertain territory was fodder for my worst side. I didn't know where anything was. I didn't know where we were supposed to be. I didn't know how long we had to wait or where we should be at any given moment. I didn't know a thing. But we learned that before the EGA ceremony, the recruits would go for one last motivational run, parading themselves in formation in their short little PT (physical training) shorts and skivvy shirts (Marine-speak for the olive t-shirt they wear under their cammies).

This was it! My first chance to catch a glimpse of Sam! *Would he look the same?* Panic rose in me as I looked frantically along the columns and rows of identical recruits, double-timing it away. Dammit! They *all* looked the same! How was I going to find him?

My heart felt like it was about to explode, and I started hyperventilating. Every nerve in my body felt exposed. I was on the verge of crying and had to accept that I wasn't going to see him yet. I'd have to wait—even longer. If I would have allowed myself to, I could have crumpled to the ground and sobbed right there.

We were instructed to head to the parade deck and sit in the bleachers behind the stenciled numbers of our recruit's platoon number. I'd already waited three months, but this wait felt interminable. Absence hadn't helped my underlying insecurities, and fearful thoughts flooded my brain. *Will I recognize him? Will he be the same Sam? Will he still be into me?* Finally, a uniform parade of khaki-clad jarheads appeared. We all scanned frantically from Marine to Marine, easily passing over short or dark-skinned ones, trying to pick Sam out of the relatively tall, white ones. But they really did all look the same.

"Is that him!?" someone asked. "No. His arms aren't hairy enough," my dad replied helpfully. Great new strategy: Look for a tall, white guy with hairy arms. That helped narrow it down. Finally, there he was! We were positioned in the bleachers directly in front of him as his platoon came to a halt, left-faced, and stood at attention. Relief. Total relief. It was real. *He* was real. My handsome Sam basically looked the same—although I had never seen him with such short hair.

With some pomp and circumstance making the moment more dramatic, the Senior Drill Instructor awarded each recruit his hard-earned EGA—the moment they transformed from recruit to United States Marine. It was a proud moment, but I just wanted the ceremony to be over so I could touch *my* Marine.

Finally, we were released. I floated from the bleachers into his arms. His stronger-than-ever arms. *At last.* Safety. Security. Love. I couldn't believe we were finally here. A true "pinch me" moment. Sam was a Marine, and I could finally see him, touch him, and look into his beautiful blue eyes. I reluctantly made way for his parents and the rest of the family to get in for a hug as well.

He took us all to the chow hall. I think we had spaghetti and meatballs as we sat outside at a picnic table. I couldn't *not* touch him. I wanted to be as close as I could. We did have to rein it in, as he was in uniform, and in uniform, there is a line that can't be crossed. You can hug and kiss hello and goodbye and hold hands, but that's pretty much it. Just sitting thigh to thigh, shoulder to shoulder, was a thrill. The warmth of his body against mine felt like home.

My memory of graduation day on Friday is blurry. It was very similar to family day, only instead of hanging out on base for a couple of hours, we finally got to take our Marine with us when they were dismissed. I was far easier to be around on graduation day. The day before had relieved twelve weeks of tension and pent-up grief, anxiety, and uncertainty.

Sam flew back with us, proudly traveling in his uniform. He was still my same Sam. Nothing had changed, yet everything had changed. Now, our life was no longer our own. He was a pawn of the United States Department of Defense, and I was along for the ride. Orders would dictate our lives. But first, we at least had his boot leave, which had been extended from five days to two weeks. That luxurious extension happened because Sam was awarded Recruiter's Assistance duty, the time when a brand-new Marine gets to help out at his local Recruiting station before continuing his next training phase—Marine Combat Training (MCT).

## FORT SILL

After three long weeks of MCT at Camp Pendleton, Sam went to Fort Sill Army Base in Lawton, Oklahoma, for his Military Occupational Specialty (MOS) school, where he would be trained as an artilleryman. He'd just missed the beginning of the five-week training cycle and was slated to be at Fort Sill for nine weeks. We'd already been apart for most of the past five months, including three straight months during boot camp. I couldn't handle any more separation and was willing to drive halfway across the country to be with my Marine.

In retrospect, this was the decision of a desperate and depressed twenty-year-old newlywed who was just beginning to understand the lack of control she would have as a military wife. It was an experience though, and I had nothing better to do with my time than follow my husband around and savor any time we could spend together.

Sam was on orders, so the Marine Corps flew him to Fort Sill. A spouse is not supposed to come along for the ride during MOS school, so I was on my own. Taking control of the situation, I found a furnished studio apartment in Lawton for less than our car payment and planned to temporarily move to Lawton until Sam completed his training.

No one, including Sam, would let me drive the 1600 miles on my own, so I did what any self-respecting grown-up did—I took my mommy. She didn't work, and she was on the team, "You're not driving halfway across the country on your own," so she and her twelve-week-old puppy, Cordy, came along. The plan was that after I was settled in, she'd fly home out of Oklahoma City, then fly back to the city again when I was ready to leave and drive back home with me. Moms, huh?

Between my mom's bad back and Cordy's tiny puppy bladder, the drive took us three very long days. I got pulled over twice but only got a speeding ticket once. Score! We drove through snow in Northern

Arizona and New Mexico, saw the famous old Route 66, and lived off fast food, Diet Coke, and Big Hunk bars.

Driving into Lawton felt like arriving on a new planet. It wasn't just the dormant winter Bermuda grass and the overall grayish-brown pallor of the city that felt surreal. I was on the precipice of something big, new, and scary. This was truly the beginning of my new life as a Marine wife, and because of my foolhardy decision, I was starting it alone. Mom was with me then, but tomorrow, she was flying out and leaving me there. Sam was just five miles away, but he wasn't accessible to me. And as I'd soon learn, the Marine Corps didn't issue him a wife. Mom and I arrived just in time to get my keys from the apartment manager and unload my belongings from my Nissan pickup. Using the MapQuest directions I'd printed before we left, I drove my mom to the Oklahoma City airport and then was officially alone on a strange new planet. Do you know that you have to order cable like a week in advance? Oops. Good thing I'd brought all ten seasons of *Friends* with me. Walking into my new apartment after dropping off Mom felt like a free fall. I was really a grown-up now, living in an apartment by myself. Even though I'd been married for seven months, I'd been living with my in-laws. This was my first apartment and my first time being alone—and boy, did I feel alone. I had a real Oklahoma adventure in my first week. There were three grocery stores in Lawton, and two of them were Walmarts. I was raised a Target girl and have never liked Walmart—but when in Lawton, do as the Lawtonians do. Not only was Walmart the place for groceries, it was the place for mail, glasses, banking, renting movies, and getting your nails done.

Not being a real girly-girl, manicures weren't a regular part of my self-care routine. But I needed human contact, and painted nails felt like an Oklahoma thing or maybe a military wife kind of thing to do. I stepped outside my apartment to head to the commerce capital of Lawton and felt like I was hit by a blow dryer. It was late February, the sky was gray-brown, and there was an oddly warm wind. Driving down the road, I saw trees whipping around and debris starting to accumulate in the streets.

I parked at the Mart and was walking across the parking lot when a woman came rushing out. It felt like I was in a movie when she raised her voice over the din of the wind, "Funnel cloud's commin'! Fifty miles away, headin' right for us!! Get to cover!" Shit! What was I supposed to do? I couldn't imagine my apartment would be all that safe. Walmart was probably my safest bet, and I sure didn't want to be alone.

I met my manicurist and told him what the parking lot lady said, but he didn't seem too bothered by it. He was halfway through my second hand when we heard the crash. "Attention all Walmart customers and staff: Code Black. Please stop what you are doing and move to the back of the store. Code Black. Stay away from the doors and move to the back of the store."

This was too real. Now I was scared. *Was Sam going to be okay? What if it was really bad and I couldn't get in touch with him?* I wished I could call him. Huddling in the back of the store between racks of shoes with my manicurist, other customers, and staff, scenes from disaster movies ran through my head. I tried to play it cool, doing my best to keep the tears from falling, but I couldn't get the movie *Twister* out of my head and kept imagining the store roof being peeled off like a sardine can.

A customer said the crash had been a shopping cart that lifted off the ground and smashed into the glass front doors. Good to know, I thought, imagining my pickup with a shopping cart embedded in its windshield. I was finally able to finish my manicure, shaken and on the verge of tears. I was more upset by the feeling of loneliness and helplessness than the experience itself, but I managed to keep it together. The funnel cloud passed, missing a direct hit on Lawton by only about ten miles, but the effects of the 100+ mph winds were everywhere. When I got to my truck, I breathed a huge sigh of relief. Though it had been hit by a cart that busted a taillight and dented the rear fender, there was no shopping cart sticking out of the windshield, and all the windows were intact. The drive back to my apartment was eerie. The wind had done significant damage, and I shuddered at the thought of the devastation an actual funnel cloud could inflict. The air was still and calm now, but everywhere were downed trees and tree limbs. The sign for the local community college—a big rectangle on two high poles—was like a twisted and mangled street creature.

I was okay, though, and my apartment was fine. Even though my truck took some damage, it was drivable, and insurance would cover it. I was still worried about Sam but beyond relieved when he finally called late in the afternoon.

"Sam!" I said. "Thank God you're okay. I've been so worried about you! What happened on base during the tornado?" "It was loud and wild, but you know how the buildings are—solid concrete," he reassured. "How are you—are you okay? Where were you?"

"I was doing my best to be a Lawtonian and went for a manicure, of all things—at Walmart." For a moment, it all hit me, and my body gave a quick shake. "Yep, it was a real adventure huddling with the Walmart staff and customers in the back of the store, surrounded by racks of shoes." Sam laughed. "Babe, you can find the positive in anything." Those afternoon calls from Sam were the relief I looked forward to every day. The earliest he could call was four in the afternoon, so each day was basically a countdown to 1600 hours. But the calls didn't always come, and I would be devastated—lonelier than ever. Luckily, Sam had good news to share early on. During one of his first calls, he said that instead of having to hang out for four weeks until the next training cycle started, they'd let him start half a week late and catch up. As long as he passed everything, we'd only be there for five weeks instead of nine. I had total faith that he'd pass, and we could soon be a real married couple living together.

Sam had weekends "off," but he usually couldn't leave the base. I was allowed to visit, though, and hang out in an open-air covered area under the barracks. We spent the weekends playing Risk, and a Marine buddy would occasionally join. We even developed a naval system that we'd be surprised to see later in the "Lord of the Rings" version of the game.

As the weeks went on, Sam's "liberty" increased. "Liberty" is Marine-speak for time allowed away from the base. This meant that sometimes, after they were dismissed for the day, he could actually leave the base as long as he was back in time for curfew at 8:00 p.m. There was even one weekend (sadly, only one) where he spent the night at the apartment with me—a small slice of heaven. Lawton doesn't have much to do, so we'd pick up some Popeye's Chicken or order pizza and just enjoy the little private time we had together in our first apartment.

The trouble with being in such a highly supervised level of training was that the Marine had zero control of his fate outside of his own behavior and performance. The days when Sam wasn't able to call or leave the base due to someone else's behavior or lack of performance left me in my gray, lonely head space. My depression from boot camp had stayed with me. I had nothing to fill my days but waiting for the call that may not come. I'd wait all day, mostly watching *Friends* or trying to read. I even got a book from Hobby Lobby and made a failed attempt to teach myself to knit. As the clock ticked closer to 1600 hours each day, my stomach got the same butterflies I used to get when we were dating. Sam was my world, and each afternoon, I'd find out if my world would be happy or crushed. Not knowing what I could count on slowly killed my innate sense of positivity. Not having control over my own life made me more armored. I did my best to focus on the positive and the temporary nature of the current circumstances. This was early training for the patience and resilience I'd need later.

A couple of weeks in, Sam and I were eating dinner at the apartment when he made a comment about me seeming distant and not myself. He was right. Just as he was learning to protect our country, I was learning to be a Marine wife and that meant protecting myself. It was the beginning of what I'd later call "deployment mode"—putting a wall of protection around my heart so I wasn't in constant pain.

"My heart can't take the ups and downs of getting to talk to you or see you," I told him. "And when the call doesn't come, or you can't come home, I have to deal with not just being disappointed, but that makes my loneliness even greater. So I guess I subconsciously built a wall to protect myself.""Oh, man, Erin," he said. "I didn't realize how hard this is for you.""I don't want to be distant, Sam, but if I don't let you in, I won't be as crushed when the phone doesn't ring or I have to take you back to the barracks."

Now, *he* was crushed. Even though he knew I wasn't, he said it felt like I was breaking up with him because the weight of what I'd just revealed hit him so hard. That was the second time I'd ever seen him cry. He knew that his choice to join the Marine Corps was causing this distance between us, and he didn't know how to fix it.

CHAPTER FIVE

# PLAYING HOUSE AND GEARING UP FOR THE FIRST DEPLOYMENT

In May 2004, Sam was assigned to Kilo Battery 3/12, attached to 2/11 out of Las Pulgas at Camp Pendleton in North San Diego County. Our dream came true when we finally got to live together as husband and wife in our own apartment! Rather than accepting base housing, we decided to live in the small town of Oceanside.

Once again, I chose an apartment based on its price and proximity to the base without ever seeing it in person. Internet rental sites weren't what they are now, but I secured us a first-floor apartment about two miles from Camp Pendleton's mainside gate and about two miles from the suburban town of Vista, where we did most of our off-base shopping.

The apartment complex was nestled in the middle of a colorful, mostly Spanish-speaking duplex neighborhood. Traversing the neighborhood was like driving through a piñata. Single buildings were split down the middle and often painted with clashing color combinations. One side might be shades of teal, the other bright yellow with hot pink trim. Most dwellings were protected by a set of stone lions, eagles, or gargoyles adorning brick pillars flanking the driveway. Our one-bedroom apartment had everything we needed—a hand-me-down mattress, Sam's old futon for a couch, and his trunk that served as our TV stand. When family came to visit, they stayed on an air mattress in our guest room, also known as our eat-in kitchen.

Living on our own for the first time (save the short bout in Oklahoma) felt a bit like playing house—maybe because we were still so young and inexperienced. We'd been married for ten months already, but this was our first time getting to set up our own place and live independently. He was the dad, and I was the mom. Any sense of homesickness turned us toward each other, seeking the comfort and care we were used to getting from our parents.

Living on a private first class's salary meant we had very little expendable income, but we made do by embracing the romanticism of being young and poor and on our own. We bought Kool-Aid instead of soda, saved plastic water bottles to painstakingly fill one at a time at water-filling stations on base, and dinner was often spaghetti, boxed macaroni and cheese, or our favorite—canned chili with nacho cheese Doritos.

Marines have to get their hair cut every week, which added up, so we invested in a $20 pair of clippers, and I figured out how to give a jarhead haircut. The first weekend of the month was payday, so we went to Great Clips in Vista. They took care of the top and showed me how to follow their template for the back and sides until the next payday. I didn't do terribly for figuring it out on my own, but after Sam was injured, this would be a skill I honed and a task I loved.

Sam was slated to deploy just four or five months after our arrival in Oceanside. We only had one car, so we decided I wouldn't work and could enjoy any time we could be together. When you live your life based on a deployment schedule—with three-day to five-week-long field operations interrupting your time at home—that time together is precious. We spent a good deal of our free time playing video games and even beat a game in a single weekend. We played tennis most weekend mornings at a local park, figuring it out as we went, but just happy to be outside playing together.

Looking back, this was a fun chapter in our lives. The stress of his first deployment loomed over us, but it also made us cherish what was most important to us—spending time together.

As his first Iraq deployment approached, we started using a credit card more liberally to enjoy experiences together, like attending Comic Con in San Diego and going to Disneyland, a first for Sam. The unspoken but understood rationale was that we may not get another chance. *Carpe diem!*

## FIRST DEPLOYMENT

Sam's first deployment was from late 2004 to mid-2005, and he participated in Operation Phantom Fury, the large-scale assault on Fallujah insurgents. This being my first deployment, as well as Sam's, I had to figure out how to do life without him and without making myself sick with worry. Commence deployment mode. I moved back home to Northern California with my parents, where I worked for a small local bank and took online classes from the University of Phoenix. I had to bump up my coping strategies from what I'd established in Fort Sill because this time, I wasn't just lonely; Sam was far away. I had seven months to get through. Seven months alone—seven months of Sam in danger.

We had seven long months to survive.

I fell asleep every night praying. I avoided the news. It was an election year and President George W. Bush was up for re-election. I had a hard time dealing with the news of the election and especially the war, so I learned to avoid it and removed myself from any conversation that went in those directions.

I once spent an evening alone in my room instead of watching *The Notebook* with my family because I just couldn't let my emotional guard down. If I let myself watch an emotional war movie with a tragic love story, I'd completely lose it. That's not deployment mode. Instead, I became a great emotion stuffer. I'm different now, but at the time, I couldn't let myself cry in front of others. Deployment mode meant emotional detachment.

Sam had a job to do, in an armored-up Humvee, with Kevlar and body armor. He was the one who called me. As little control as he had over how frequently he got to call, I had *zero*. He didn't experience the same emotional detachment I did. If anything, thoughts of me back at home spurred him on. Meanwhile, I was home trying not to think of the war, trying not to think about Sam at all except for when I wrote my daily letter.

Deployment mode meant that I needed to find a way to put my head down, stay busy, and focus on myself to keep my mind off him. And the danger he was in. Working part-time at the bank and taking classes helped my days stay busy and structured. And Sam's brother, Donny, was a great balm to my pain and loneliness. We both were there for each other because Sam was our person. Neither of us knew what to do without him, so we stuck together.

New comic books were released on Wednesdays, so Donny and I had a weekly date at A-1 Comics. We'd usually pick up Subway on the way home, then hang out reading our new comics together before settling into an evening with the *Simpsons* or *Family Guy*. One of these evenings was the annual "Simpson's Treehouse of Horror Halloween" episode. Based on the episode's spoof, the ending credits rolled to the theme song from the late-80s, early-90s sitcom *Perfect Strangers*. Donny and I rolled with laughter, a welcome relief from my pent-up stress.

To my utter devastation, early the next morning, I missed a call from Sam. I was getting ready for work and didn't hear the phone ring over the water running. He tried both my cell and house phone, but before I could catch the second attempt, he was gone. He then called Donny, who called me as soon as they hung up.

I was destroyed. Donny did what he could to ease my mind and relay Sam's updates and his love, but I missed him too much for this to help. My phone was my lifeline to Sam, and I couldn't believe I'd been so stupid not to bring it with me to the bathroom. From that moment on, I'd never be away from my phone again.

I was the kind of upset where the slightest thought of that missed call would send me back into a soggy, hyperventilating mess. Fortunately or unfortunately, I still had to go to work. It was a tiny bank branch inside a Sun City retirement community, and the staff was close. So when

I arrived at the bank red faced and puffy eyed, my co-workers, who were like aunties to me, knew something was wrong. And, of course, I crumbled as soon as they asked. My boss, Pat, was a Marine wife herself. Her husband had long since retired, but she knew my pain, and she knew how painfully young I was.

I somehow made it through the morning. Heading out on my lunch break, I got the sweetest surprise—Donny had left me a voicemail, singing the entire *Perfect Strangers* theme song to me. I cried, but at least they were tears of laughter, joy, and love for my brother-in-law. I can't think of a better way to cheer anyone up. If you're feeling down, look it up on YouTube. I promise you'll feel better.

A phone call I didn't miss started with Donny inviting me to celebrate my twenty-first birthday with him. He was twenty-two and took me to the closest watering hole, the Corner Pocket pool hall. This wasn't my first drinking experience, but it was my first with an entire bar of options to choose from. Let me tell you, not mixing your alcohol is an important lesson to learn.

A while after we got back to my in-laws', I excused myself to the bathroom to expel some of the poison I'd ingested. Sometime later, Donny came to check on me, and he found me asleep, kneeling in front of the toilet, my head resting on a towel hanging from the towel rack. He helped me back to Sam's and my old room, where I spent the night on the floor because the bed spun too much and I didn't want my stomach erupting onto the mattress.

The next morning, Donny dropped me off at my parent's house, and I barely kept myself composed for the five-minute drive. No sooner had I walked in the door when Sam called. "Hang on," I said. "We're about to share something very special." Carefully setting my phone on the bathroom counter, I tossed my cookies. "I'm holding your hair back in spirit!" Sam yelled. That's true love.

## FIRST HOMECOMING

Seven months is a long time to be apart. It's an even longer time to be at war in a state of constant vigilance. People come back from war different. I'd heard this and seen this in the movies and was so scared that Sam would be changed. He'd seen combat and significant trauma. What did that mean for who he was and how he'd relate to me? The hardest part was that he'd had all those experiences without me. His time in Iraq was shared with his Marine buddies, not with me. So, in addition to just missing him, I experienced almost a fear of missing out. As many stories as he'd tell me, I would never share those experiences. He had something completely separate from me, and that threatened "SamnErin." Now I wondered, where did I fit into the life of the Sam who had been to war?

I was a nervous wreck when I stayed overnight on base again with Meaghann and John. The wait to drive to Las Pulgas, Sam's unit's area on base, felt endless. All day long, I pictured the buses pulling up and Sam walking off and into my arms.

As I stood on the basketball courts at Las Pulgas, I felt like I would burst with anticipation. It was a combination of anxiety about what he would be like and the all-too-familiar butterflies from when we were dating.

Like most things we worry about and build up in our heads, I really had nothing to worry about. Sam was Sam, and he couldn't have been happier to see me. My only memory of the reunification was seeing each other and being quickly wrapped up in his arms, being held tight like he'd never left. Home. He was safely back at home, and I was safely in his arms.

# ROADSIDE BOMB ON OCEANSIDE BLVD.

We decided together that we should give Sam a week or two to adjust to being back safe at home before he started driving. In Iraq, personal vehicles couldn't come within 100 meters of American military convoys, and anything could be an improvised explosive device (IED). That distance was unimaginable in crowded southern California, and we didn't want any overreaction from him to cause an accident. Sam had been in multiple firefights (Marine-speak for exchanging gunfire with the enemy). As I mentioned, he'd been in Operation Phantom Fury, the large-scale assault to drive insurgents out of Fallujah. He'd traveled thousands of miles across Iraq, scouring the barren land for anything that could be an IED.

The day after he returned from Iraq, Sam and I were driving down Oceanside Blvd., the main road between our apartment and the I-5 freeway, when he spotted a potential IED. We were at a crawl in front of Ralph's grocery store, waiting to enter the freeway on-ramp. At the bus stop in front of Ralph's was a crumpled-up paper bag. "IED!" Sam said forcefully. He was trained for this and didn't panic, but he instantly started looking for an escape route. Placing my hand on his thigh, I reminded him of where we were and that we were safe. "There's probably an empty bottle of booze in the bag. A lot of unhoused people hang around this area."

Sam saw the logic, but I could see that it took a while for his heart rate to slow and for the adrenaline still pumping through his system to subside. This was the first time I'd had to adopt a calm, soothing voice and assure him that everything was okay. We were safe. What I didn't yet know was that this reaction was his first episode of PTSD.

## PTSD

Anger and frustration with work. Trouble sleeping. My palpable exhale and relaxation when Sam got in the car. Besides being in a state of constant vigilance for seven months, he had watched American contractors in armored-up Hummers die. He'd helped Navy corpsman treat the sucking chest wound of one of the contractors who ultimately didn't make it. Sam's PTSD took a few forms, but the most disruptive were claustrophobia and agoraphobia. We commonly took a shower together on Saturday and Sunday mornings, but every now and then, he'd panic, saying, "Move! I have to get out!" His hyper-vigilance from the deployment remained even though he was safe at home, and I became his de-escalation therapist, helping him calm down in the evening.

SeaWorld offered free admission tickets once a year to active-duty military and up to four dependents. We went three years in a row, but the last time, on a rare weekday he had off from work, Sam panicked. Despite there being a small amount of people there, he was sweating profusely in beautiful seventy-degree weather, and his head was on a swivel. About thirty minutes in, he announced we had to leave. He couldn't do it. Sometimes PTSD just happens like that for no apparent reason.

When we went home for the holidays, he'd disappear. He'd escape the noise and energy of so many people talking in a relatively small space to go for a walk instead or find a quiet room to sit.

Little did we know how much trauma would become part of our daily lives.

## JAPAN DEPLOYMENT

At the time Sam was in the Marine Corps, Marines deployed in seven-month stints—deployed for seven months, home for seven months. When his home stint was over, Sam deployed for a second time on a Marine Expeditionary Unit (MEU), where the Marines go out on ships with the Navy and kind of patrol a portion of the globe. Sam's home port was Okinawa, Japan, from where they also went to Guam, Korea, the Philippines, and Thailand.

I sure handled my second deployment experience better than the first. I went back to my job at the country club and re-enrolled in community college. Deployment timing allowed me to get a full semester in this time, so I took a full load of fifteen units. I'd recently begun working out on base and joined a local gym as well so I could reach my goal of getting into the best shape of my life by the time Sam came home.

School determined my work schedule, and they both determined my workout schedule. That strict routine helped with my mental health. The routine and attention to improving myself both academically and physically gave me an important area of focus outside of Sam.

At that time, I lived in a two-bedroom apartment with Sam's mom. She'd just recently left my father-in-law and moved into one of the apartments she managed. Donny and I were the family envoys—I got custody of Mom, and Donny had Dad. As the seven months wound down, I wasn't as afraid of the ending of the deployment as I had been the time before. Of course, it helped that Sam wasn't at war this time, but I'd also been through the reunification process and could be more excited than nervous this time around.

But Sam's experience of this deployment was far worse than mine. Marines don't have much to do on a Navy ship, and he hated all the waiting around. He said he spent his time on the ship working out, reading, and playing video games. Meanwhile, I was at the gym as much as possible. I got the smallest and leanest I've ever been as an adult, and he got the biggest and buffest he'd ever been.

Sam said that midway through the MEU, he experienced the worst four days of his life. They were on their way to an island in the Philippines to do some training with the Philippine Marines when an earthquake caused a mudslide, burying the village of Leyte. Out of the three ships in the MEU, two continued on to the scheduled training while the Marines went to Leyte for disaster relief. People had been buried alive. The Marines spent four days clearing roads and recovering bodies from the sucking mud, but the only survivor they found was a chicken.

They slept in wall-less tents on the beach, only a foam mat and a poncho between them and the mud that had claimed the lives of so many. It rained relentlessly and rained sideways, so the tent was more a suggestion of cover than anything protective. Then Sam woke one morning to discover his feet had been in an ant hill, and he was covered in hundreds of bites.

As much violence as he'd experienced in Iraq, those four days in the Philippines were the most trying and most upsetting to him. He'd seen dead bodies. He'd even killed when engaged in combat in Iraq. But these were innocent people. They weren't able to roll in and roll out of town like you do on a convoy. They were there for days with the surviving villagers who'd just lost family, homes, and businesses.

The experience would play a crucial role in Sam ending up in Iraq for the second time.

Regardless of the type of deployment, it sucked, and so did the communication. It was better when he was on the MEU than in Iraq, but not much. In order to talk, he had to wait in line for a phone at the phone center, then had a fifteen- or twenty-minute limit for the call we both needed so much.

His most frequent calls came on the MEU when they were at their home base at Camp Hansen in Okinawa, Japan. It was almost decadent because sometimes he even got to call two or three days in a row. This was a rare luxury, though, because sometimes it would be as many as three or four *weeks* between calls.

One time, during his first tour in Iraq, Sam wasn't able to call for several weeks. They'd been out on a mission, and when they arrived back to Camp Ramadi, some sort of incident made the phone center shut down temporarily. Not wanting to leave me hanging any longer, he did the only thing he could think to do—I came home from work to find a vase filled with the same orchids we wore as leis at our wedding, along with a card from Sam. What a guy! The gesture made me miss him even more, but it also filled me with the reassurance I needed. Reassurance that he was still out there—still safe—still mine. When we did actually get to talk, it was mostly the same mundane things couples talk about; only his day at work may have involved mortars and a firefight, while mine still involved the country club and community college tasks.

After the excruciating experience of missing his phone call during the first deployment, Sam always called in the middle of my night so I wouldn't miss him. I constantly slept with my phone near my bed, always on call. But no matter how important the phone call, sleep can overwhelm it. Depending on where I was in my sleep cycle when the phone rang, sometimes even the excitement and adrenaline rush of hearing his voice could barely wake me out of my sleepy stupor. I'd have to walk around the house to properly wake up and not waste our precious conversation.

As much as my deployment mode was in full effect, I could still give myself to him on our calls, those single rays of sunlight peeking through an otherwise cloud-filled sky. Just for the space of that call, I could be open and real.

One time, when he called, I was house-sitting for my aunt and uncle, enjoying the pool while taking care of their dogs. Lying on their bed in my bikini, playing with my belly button ring, the subject of kids came up. We'd always planned on waiting until our late 20s and definitely until he was out of the Marines, but in that call, we decided to at least entertain the idea of scooting up the timeline by a few years.

When I look back at these calls, they remind me of our dating years, spending hours together on the phone after school. As few and far between as the deployment calls were, I'm so glad we had them. It kept a hint of normalcy and connection that letter writing, though romantic, just didn't provide.

## HOMECOMING WITH STEVE AND A DISLOCATED THUMB

Sam's arrival home from his second deployment was all the more special, with the impending birth of Steve and Shi, our best friends' first baby. Steve and Sam had previously been in the same unit when Steve was the driver of Sam's Humvee for their first deployment to Iraq.

After that deployment, we'd gotten very close. Shi was a Marine as well, but she was stationed in Okinawa, Japan. It would take several months after the boys came home from Iraq for Shi to be transferred to Camp Pendleton. In the meantime, suffering from PTSD and living alone, Steve spent most weekends with us, even if it was just for the night. Nights were the worst for him, and just knowing we were in the next room eased some of his distress.

Because Steve and Shi had just been reunited, Steve was able to transfer to a different battery (Marine-speak for an artillery company), one that wasn't about to deploy. Shi got pregnant a couple of months before Sam deployed, so he was making it back for the baby's birth—just in time.

The Marines from Camp Pendleton fly into March Air Reserve Base in Riverside County and take buses for the hour-long trip south to Camp Pendleton. Families of returning Marines had to wait at the basketball courts for the buses to arrive. It was grueling to wait even more after seven long months of separation. So I called Steve when I got there, and he met me out on the courts. I hoped that having a friend would ease my nerves and distract me during the agonizing wait.

Whenever Sam deployed, I always went back up north to Sacramento, so I hadn't seen Steve in seven months. After greeting each other with a big hug, my first question was about the baby. When's he coming? I asked. To my astonishment and delight, Shi had gone into labor that morning.

I couldn't believe Steve was at work, and even more unbelievable, so was Shi! Like us, Steve and Shi lived off base in Oceanside. Camp Pendleton is huge, and being a Marine isn't like any other job where you can just hang out at home waiting for your wife's labor contractions to send you to the hospital. It made the most sense for them both to go to work on base, so when she was ready to go to the hospital, Steve would be a lot closer than if he had to drive home. Steve and I were both beyond excited but tense as hell, him awaiting the birth of his first child and me the homecoming of the love of my life. Having someone to wait with made the wait more bearable, keeping the irrational questions about whether Sam would be the same or whether or not he still loves me at bay.

Then Steve's phone rang. It was Shi. It was time. Sam hadn't arrived yet, but baby boy Marquez was on his way. Steve's energy went from basically calm to bordering on frantic. He probably couldn't have told you his own name. I gave him a big hug and sent him off to go have his baby, saying that I'd have Sam call him later to check in, and we'd see them—all three of them— soon.

Shortly after the father-to-be left, the buses came in. But of course it wasn't as simple as Sam walking down the steps into my arms. First, they had to get the gear off the buses, then assemble into formation before finally being dismissed to their families. "Hurry up and wait" is the unofficial Marine Corps motto. I've experienced two of these homecomings, but I still can't give you a drop of detail about what is said to the Marines or the families before they're dismissed. I was too busy frantically searching for Sam among the cammie-clad Marines, heart in my throat, stomach in knots.

Dismissed! The frenzy begins! Camouflage flashes and squeals of delight, laughter, sobs, but—where's my Marine? The fist-clenching of my insides tightened and twisted as my panic rose, but then... there he is! His beautiful blue eyes locked on me, and suddenly, I was in his arms being whirled around. Those lips! Oh, how I missed those lips. Let's go home.

For this stint in Oceanside, I'd secured an apartment in the same complex we'd lived in before, chosen not for its amenities but because it felt like home. Unlike most of Southern California, this place had grass, evergreen trees, a variety of multi-colored shrubs, along with the expected towering palm trees. Being from Northern California, I needed greenery. The brown and sage-green palette of SoCal foliage did nothing but depress me. And unless you're looking directly at the ocean (and it's not May or June, in which case the view is obscured by a thick blanket of marine layer), I'm sorry, but SoCal is ugly.

To be completely moved in and unpacked when Sam arrived, I'd driven the 385 miles from Citrus Heights down to Oceanside three times in the week before his arrival. When your life and marriage exist in seven-month intervals, there's no time to waste.

A friend drove with me for the first trip, taking as much furniture and as many boxes as my Nissan Frontier pick-up could carry. We slept on an air mattress and took the time to get burritos from my favorite Mexican fast-food place, Eribertos. After a body surf at Oceanside City Beach, we drove the 385 miles north again within 24 hours.

Two days later, Donny came down with me, helping me with some of the bigger furniture. This time, we stayed the night and then headed north the next morning. The last trip I made solo, relying on Meaghann and John to help me unload the last couple of pieces of furniture. When we weren't heaving furniture, all I could think was that Sam would be with me for the next trip north.

Sam, weary from seven months mostly at sea and several days of travel, walked into a completely furnished, unpacked, and decorated apartment. All we had to do was unload his gear in the hall closet, and we would be settled. But first things first, it had been seven months.

Later that hot July day, we decided to take a swim. We'd been drinking, and just after I'd changed into my swimsuit, Sam walked in and threw me on the bed. I landed with one arm over my head, and for some unknown reason, drunken Sam thought it would be fun to spit in my armpit. I know! What the hell?!

Sensing his mistake and my playful fury, he backed away and assumed a defensive posture. I jumped up and swiftly punched him in the arm, only...DAMMIT! My thumb! In my own drunkenness, my aim was askew, and instead of hitting him squarely, I was off by an inch or two, delivering most of the punch with my thumb rather than a balled-up fist.

I dislocated it. But thank God I was drunk because without thinking, I popped it right back into place. Sam went to get me ice, but we'd just refilled the ice trays, having used all the ice for our cocktails. We didn't even have any frozen food in the freezer to help with the swelling, so we might as well head down to the pool. Although the cold, still water felt good on my swelling thumb, swimming didn't last very long because even the gentle movement of the water killed me.

The next day, I couldn't move my thumb, but we had a baby boy to meet. Isaiah Marquez was born on July 14, 2006, the day Uncle Sam came home from Japan. I couldn't believe how tiny he was. Most mind-boggling of all, though, was the reality that Steve and Shi, who were younger than Sam and I, were responsible for this precious, tiny little life. They were the first of our friends to have a baby, so this was the first time I'd ever considered the absurdity of twenty-year-old knuckleheads being parents. Don't get me wrong, Steve and Shi had their heads screwed on straight, but Sam and I were still kids! We spent our free time drinking and playing video games.

Sam wouldn't hold the baby, but he couldn't stop looking at little Isaiah. Instead, he stood behind me, peering over my shoulder to get a good look. But he was scared. He'd never held a baby, and today, standing on the cold, hard hospital floor wasn't going to be his first time. It wouldn't be until Isaiah was almost crawling, enticing him by playfully pulling at Uncle Sam's sock, that he held that baby for the first time. Sam had loved Isaiah before, but when he finally held that little body to his chest, I thought his heart was going to explode. Shi and I looked at each other and smiled. There is nothing hotter to a woman than a man who loves kids.

# CHAPTER SIX

# FINAL DEPLOYMENT

Sam was about to deploy for the third time in three years. Although he was slated to separate (Marine-speak for get out) from the Marines in October, he would now have to extend his contract by three months in order to return to Iraq for his final deployment.

That out-of-control feeling from year one of Marine Corps life returned. I felt dubious, but what could I do? There was nothing to do but support him. Even though I had a bad feeling about this final deployment, I was also weirdly at peace with it. This was our third rodeo, and I was resigned to take it like the salty ole twenty-three-year-old Marine wife I was. I couldn't change that it was happening, but I could try to make the most of the time we had before deployment.

In fact, my lack of emotion concerned Sam. Reminiscent of our conversation back in Oklahoma, he confronted me with his worry that I wasn't worried—even hurt that I wasn't a basket case. I wasn't demonstrating the same fear, anxiety, and high emotional state I had leading up to his previous deployments because I was well trained at this point. The separation and all the emotions around it were old hat.

But I even asked myself why it was so easy. This certainly felt better than being miserable. As the departure date got closer, though, it got harder. Even being intimate didn't feel right. We were in pain from anticipating him leaving, so engaging in pleasure didn't feel right. We really just wanted to cuddle and be near each other, taking in the feeling of closeness while we could.

Most of all, though, my brain was protecting me from the emotions that were really there, just as I had learned to do way back at Fort Sill. That ability to compartmentalize served me well— for a time. It would come back to bite me in later years.

What my mind was most focused on was life after the Marine Corps. We both felt very similarly to our eighteen-year-old selves. The world was our oyster, but we didn't know what to do with it. The only thing that had changed in the past four years was our age. We had, of course, matured, but our position in life was the same. And soon, we'd be starting over as civilians.

Our plan was to move to Reno, Nevada. It was less than two hours from home, but the Sierra Nevada mountain range would still separate us from our parents, giving us the sense of autonomy we craved. We'd get jobs, go to community college, and establish Nevada residency so we could eventually attend the University of Nevada, Reno, a good school at an even better price. I planned to study nutrition, as I had spent the previous deployments getting in great shape, and it seemed to align with my interests. Sam really didn't know what he wanted to do, so he'd probably study business. Again, we were at this crossroads where all we really knew was that whatever came next, we would be in it together.

# THE LAST GOODBYE

As always, we lived it up in the last couple of months before his deployment, using our credit card to pay for experiences and memories. We didn't even worry about it because I'd pay those off and save money during the deployment.

Sam was a non-commissioned officer (NCO) now, which meant he got to carry a pistol on deployment as well as his M-16. For fun, and in preparation to qualify at the range on the pistol, we went to Iron Sights, an indoor gun range in Oceanside. At first, it was just the two of us, then his dad and brother went with us when they came to visit. Later, we went to Medieval Times in Anaheim, where we had a blast drinking rum and Cokes and "mead" and watching our knight dominate.

In preparation for the deployment, we moved most of our stuff back to Sacramento, keeping only the essential items in the apartment because I'd have to carry them when I made the final trip back north solo.

We lived mostly off take-out and happy-hour dinners at our local pub. Hooligans was just across the street from our apartment and was owned by a retired Marine and his English wife. Every day at 4:00 p.m., they put out the food of the day. As long as you were drinking, the food was free, and we loved our favorite—bangers and mash.

But the word was out that Sam was leaving soon, so our money was no good. The old timers bought us pitchers and single beers right and left. If we had a beer in front of us and somebody wanted to buy us a drink, they'd give us a wooden token, setting us up for the next round.

But food is more than nutrition, and we had a thing about our comfort drink, chocolate milk. One day, when Sam was homesick and frustrated as he waited to come home from Okinawa, I told him he needed Vitamin D, so he should take some chocolate milk and a book and go sit in the sun after we hung up. It worked. When he called the next day, he was in a much better mood.

Another time, I picked him up from work on a Friday afternoon, and we were both picking and sniping at each other for no reason, which was really out of the norm for us. He wanted to rent *Mortal Kombat*, so we started at Hollywood Video, but they only had *Mortal Kombat: Annihilation*, the sequel. The same unfortunate result at Blockbuster. Meanwhile, we were just being jerks to each other for no reason. We didn't end up renting anything.

The ride home was awkwardly quiet. When we got back inside our apartment, I went to the bathroom and decided it was a great time for an elaborate skincare routine. Sam had gone to lie down on our bed, no doubt wanting to talk it out, but I was being petty and wasn't ready to give him the satisfaction.

When I finished in the bathroom, instead of joining him in the bedroom, I went to the living room and sat in front of the TV. Sam eventually joined me, but we continued our hostile silence. It was so stupid because we weren't even mad at each other for any reason. We were both just in pissy, antagonistic moods.

Finally, I said, "Want some chocolate milk? I hear vitamin D is great for PMS."

"Sure," he said, following me to the kitchen. And just like that, before we were done stirring in the Nesquik, we were all better, holding each other in a long hug. Chocolate milk saved the day yet again.

So, when the final days before his last deployment came, we drank *a lot* of chocolate milk. I have a sweet picture of him sitting on the couch the day he left, drinking his chocolate milk from a red solo cup.

We spent that last day, March 25, 2007, making the most of our dwindling time together. First, we went to breakfast, then met Steve, Shi, and baby Isaiah at Pizza Port in Carlsbad. We spent the evening leading up to his 10:00 p.m. drop-off just being together. His warmth, his weight, his smell, his scratchy face. I was doing my best to take it all in so it would hold me over for the next seven months. I bet Sam felt the same. At 10:00 p.m., I dropped him off at the same basketball courts we normally had our reunions. It was a tearful goodbye. We couldn't hold each other tight enough. And I never wanted to let go, to get back in the car, to drive away from the love of my life. The unspoken knowledge that this could be our last goodbye was palpable.

I spent that night in the apartment alone and made the drive back home, crying and rocking out to the new System of a Down album.

## THE FIRST PHONE CALL

This time, deployment mode for me mostly consisted of being either drunk or hungover. I stayed with my parents but spent most of my time with Donny and his girlfriend, Brandi. Soon, I went to work for Brandi at Dimple Records, a local (and now defunct) new and used record store. We'd go back to my father-in-law's after work, where Donny, Brandi, and I spent the late evenings drinking rum and Cokes and playing Wii Sports, Apples to Apples, or Mad Libs while they smoked on the back patio.

One major commonality among Donny, Brandi, Sam, and I was our love of Harry Potter, even though I didn't start reading the books until after the fourth movie came out. I'd loved all the movies, and I was finally ready to board the Hogwarts Express myself. I read books one to four in quick succession, clamoring to get to the brand-new-to-me material of books five and six. Sam caught the bug as well and read the series right behind me. He was a faster reader than I, but he had the disadvantage of going to work every day. I got to stay home and read. We finished the six books in the series in record time and then had about eighteen months to wait for the final installment of Harry's story. We all became Harry Potter super-nerds, watching the movies over and over, reading the books (in our best English accents) to each other, and playing various trivia games. And, of course, we had drinking games to accompany and enhance all these activities. Sadly, Sam was deployed for the release of the fifth movie in July 2007, but I'd send him book seven. Donny, Brandi, her siblings, and I attended the midnight release party at Barnes & Noble in Sacramento, California. We embraced all the fanfare and participated in various wizarding activities: being sorted into our respective Hogwarts houses (I'm a proud Gryffindor), wand-making, and getting polaroids with a life-size Harry Potter cutout (I still have mine).

At the stroke of midnight, the cash registers were open, and we bought our books—in fact, I bought one pre-ordered special edition in a slip-case and two standard hardbacks, one for me and one to send to Sam. But nothing was going to delay my delight, and when I got home near 1:00 a.m., I set straight to reading for a good hour. But I didn't want to waste any of the books from being too tired, so I went to sleep with plans to rise early and read all day. Sure enough, I spent the entire next day reading in my room, only stopping to go out for coffee (and taking Harry with me) and ordering a pizza, grease stains be damned.

Still awake at 1:00 a.m. the morning after the morning of the release, I was just starting the epilogue when my phone rang. It was Sam calling from Iraq! Unlike our normal middle-of-the-night calls, this time, I was wide awake.

"Know what I'm doing right now?"

"What?"

"Reading the seventh Harry Potter."

"Don't tell me anything! Send it to me right away!"

But it was the wee hours of Sunday, so I'd have to wait until Monday to send off his most-anticipated care package of the deployment. We talked for the fifteen to twenty minutes his turn at the phone station in Camp Ramadi allowed, and then both hung up on a huge high.

First thing Monday morning, I was at the post office sending Sam his copy full of little notes from me and the Polaroid of me with the Harry Potter cutout. I couldn't wait to talk after he read it. But life in the muggle world would have to do for now.

The next day was just another mildly hungover Tuesday morning after about five hours of sleep and another trip to Noah's Bagels for an everything bagel with cream cheese and a coffee. Just as I was stepping into the street, I noticed the license plate of a pewter Chevy Tahoe with a pretty blonde driver—Purple Heart. Was the Purple Heart hers? Her husband's? Dad's?

Purple Hearts are awarded to those wounded or killed while serving.

When I was in deployment mode, I made a conscious effort not to see things like this—evidence of a reality that could be. I avoided the news. This was Sam's third deployment, and I was a seasoned Marine wife who knew what I needed to do to get through yet another separation. Alcohol helped with that during this deployment so I could focus on myself and shut out the world. I wouldn't normally ruminate on the circumstances behind a woman driving a vehicle with Purple Heart plates. But that day, I did.

I never thought I was cool enough to work at a record store, but there I was, working a mid-shift. Brandi, my future sister-in-law, was my boss, and it was a blast getting to work together, even if she was cooler than me.

About an hour into my shift, I was straightening up the shelves when a buzz from my back pocket stopped me. Oops. Forgot to put my phone in my purse in the back room. I checked the number, and my heart sank. Shit. (760) 725-xxxx. Camp Pendleton.

Quickly walking to the backroom, as I answered the phone, I heard, "Mrs. Nichols?" *No, no, no, no, no, no, no. This couldn't be happening.* It was the leave-behind officer (Marine-speak for an officer from the unit who stays on base) from Sam's unit. Sam had been injured. He told me the few details he knew: We lost four guys on July 24th, 2007—three Marines and a Navy Corpsman. Sam was unconscious with a broken arm and leg.

The Humvee in front of Sam's had been hit by a remote-activated IED, killing Doc Daniel Noble, Corporal Heath McCrae, and Corporal Matthew Zindars. Sam, as vehicle commander, directed his driver to respond to get to their guys. Then, a second IED exploded just behind Sam. Lance Corporal Robert Lynch was sitting behind him and was killed instantly. It was three days before our fourth wedding anniversary.

I could barely breathe and almost threw up on the spot. My first thoughts were of Sam's emotional state. *How would he deal with the death of his buddies? What did the officer mean by "unconscious"?* I grabbed my purse, blurted out that Sam had been hurt, and left the building. It would take me ten years to get the courage to walk back in.

Numb, I drove straight to my mother-in-law's office. Kelley was the leasing manager at the apartments where we lived together during the last deployment, and her now-husband, Jose, as well as some residents, were in the office with her. I can't imagine the look on my face but only know that I managed to calmly ask her if she could meet me upstairs as soon as possible. The worst part of this horrific day was having to tell the news to our families and people who loved Sam. Kelley and Jose met me upstairs, where I choked out the news through tears and a strangled throat. I spent several hours with her, long enough that everyone would be at home together, so I would only have to say it once more. Then I went to my father-in-law's to tell him and Donny. My father-in-law called his oldest son Marty.

The next day, Donny went with me to tell my parents. My parents thought of Sam as their own son, and I think it was harder to tell my parents than Sam's. But after we all accepted what happened, I felt like I needed to be with Sam's family, so I stayed with Donny and my father-in-law until we left to be with Sam. Donny, Brandi, and I tried distracting ourselves with our usual Wii Sports, MadLibs, and

Apples to Apples, but the pain was too much. The "in a coma" card from Apples to Apples used to be one of our trump cards. Now, we removed it from the box.

## THE NEXT CALL

Finally, Thursday morning around 7:15 a.m. Pacific daylight time, the phone rang. An Air Force doctor calling from Landstuhl Army Medical Hospital announced that Sam had arrived safely in Germany. He was stable but in a coma and might never wake up. My heart felt six feet under, my body too heavy to move.

Shortly thereafter, I got another call from the leave-behind officer at Camp Pendleton, arranging travel for me and up to two family members who the military would fly to be with Sam. The rest of the family could fly out on the dime of various charities.

We had the choice to leave that day, arrive in Germany on Saturday morning, and then have to turn around and fly to Bethesda, Maryland, on Sunday. Or we could wait, and all fly out on Sunday. Waiting around was the worst part, but there was a bigger pressure—the chance we could lose Sam before then or that he wouldn't be stable enough to fly on Sunday. The choice was easy.

Donny and I flew out of Sacramento at 3:00 p.m. that afternoon. But because I was first issued my passport as a minor and hadn't gotten it renewed, we had to fly to D.C. for an emergency-issue passport before we could continue on to Germany. We had a several-hour layover in Denver before finally landing at Dulles International Airport in Washington, D.C. As was everything, traveling was miserable. We had long layovers, and the emergency nature of our trip triggered my old anxiety-induced vomiting—the same vomiting that had made me drop to ninety-two pounds in high school. Once again, I could hardly eat. A bite or two into something, and I'd feel like I was going to be sick. Sometimes, I was; sometimes, it passed. Donny saved my leftovers to eat later on the plane and tried to encourage me to eat what I could. Pretzel snack bags on the plane were all I could stomach—save for a bite of a sandwich here and there. My pants were falling off me within a week.

Waiting in airports was almost as bad as waiting at home, but at least we were en route. I tried to read *Eragon*, by Christopher Paolini, book one of a fantasy series I would eventually read aloud to Sam. Even though I would have given anything to be living anyone's life but my own— bring on the fictitious dragons and villains!—I couldn't focus enough to be taken away to their fantasy world. I wasn't ready to face reality, nor could I concentrate sufficiently to grasp that sweet relief. We arrived at the airport around 6:30 a.m. eastern standard time on Friday, where a young Marine drove us to the Naval Annex. A woman was waiting for us, ready to take my passport photo and fill in the information she needed. I looked like hell. She got out some blankets and told Donny and me to lie down and try to sleep while she and the young Marine went to the State Department to get my passport. We tried.

An hour or two later, they were back, but we still hadn't slept. We headed back to Dulles to wait some more. We didn't leave for Germany until that afternoon, so there was plenty of time to not eat and not read, question my life and my future, and attempt to hold it together. I'm so glad Donny was with me. Our dry and dark senses of humor made us good companions. Though we initially bonded as friends through Sam, during his boot camp and first two deployments, we had become brother and sister.

## INJURIES

Sam's injuries were as follows:

- Right fibula fracture (missing 3 inches) (shin would require skin graft)
- Right calf half blown off
- Right hip and buttock missing significant flesh (required skin graft)
- Significant lacerations to low back
- Burns on lower back and right hip
- Broken elbow (required pins)
- Broken humerus (non-displaced)
- Ruptured spleen (a portion had lodged itself in lower lobe of left lung)
- Broken ribs
- Collapsed right lung (required multiple chest tubes)
- Broken neck (fractures of facets of C3 and C4 vertebrae; no spinal cord injury)
- Traumatic Brain Injury (diffuse axonal injury; non-surgical blast injury)

After an excruciatingly long overnight flight filled with drunken German teenagers, we were met at the Frankfurt Airport by another Marine liaison. We hoped for a cool German car for the ride from Frankfurt to Landstuhl but instead got stuck with a navy blue Ford Taurus, exactly like Donny's car.

It was now Saturday morning, July 28, 2007, around 7:00 a.m. Central European Summer Time. We were finally close to seeing Sam. In Pacific daylight time, it was the late hours of our fourth wedding anniversary.

Landstuhl's overcast sky was like a light gray blanket draping across the world. Donny and I were incredibly jet-lagged, sleep-deprived, and emotionally exhausted, and the sky did little to orient us. The hallways of Landstuhl Hospital were eerily quiet—like we were somewhere we shouldn't be. Then we saw Sam for the first time.

What did they do to his hair? My jarhead had a buzz cut, and there were two medical things coming out of his head at the hairline. One was a bolt—yeah, like Frankenstein's monster—which measured intracranial pressure. The other was a drain to remove accumulated blood, which could raise the intracranial pressure.

But it was the shaved head that threw me. I'd never seen Sam without hair on top. His face was perfect. It hadn't been injured, and save the buzz cut and the tubes, he looked like my beautiful Sam.

Throughout all the grueling hours of travel, I was scared beyond belief. But seeing him in the flesh eased some of the pain and fear. I could see him! Touch him! The blurry facts of his injuries faded as I looked at his perfect face.

We met the doctor I'd spoken to on the phone Thursday morning. He explained the diffuse axonal injury, the type of brain injury Sam had sustained from the percussion of the IED blast, was similar to what happens when a baby is shaken.

There wasn't any large area of blood that could be evacuated, but instead, he had pinpoint-sized areas of bleeding throughout his brain. That meant they couldn't fix it with surgery, so we'd just have to wait and see. Though Sam was in the lowest form of coma (near brain-dead) you can be in, he was medically stable. So we were slated to medevac back to the States the next day.

A nurse gave us a tour of Sam's body and wounds, something I never expected to need regarding my own husband's body. He explained what each of the tubes, wires, and dressings were for: the ventilator was breathing for Sam via the tube in his mouth, and the tube in his nose was for nutrition.

I hardly took anything in but the rise and fall of his chest. I knew he wasn't breathing on his own, but as long as his chest rose and fell, he was alive, and there was a chance.

Eventually, Donny and I went to our room at Fisher House, showered, and took a nap, finally able to really rest after seeing Sam. With the overcast sky and not being accustomed to the later sunset of the more northern latitude, I woke Donny up in a panic, thinking we'd slept all afternoon and all night. But the 9:00 p.m. sky looked exactly the same as it had at 7:00 a.m., and we still had ten hours before we left for the States.

With an elephant on my chest and a cannonball running through my gut, we headed back over to watch Sam breathe for a while before returning to our room and watching *Rocky* in German. After more jet-lag-fighting sleep, we got up for the next leg of the adventure. Donny returned to Frankfurt with our Marine Liaison to fly commercial to D.C., while I joined Sam on the medevac.

CHAPTER SEVEN

# RETURNING TO THE STATES

As planned, the Sunday after Sam's injury, we headed back to the States. The Air Force flight crew—the doctor was a Major, the nurse was a Captain, and the respiratory therapist (RT) was a Technical Sergeant—arrived at the hospital and began setting Sam up for transport. Every tube, wire, and device had to be switched over from the hospital setup to their mobile setup. Accustomed to the very formal Marine Corps, it threw me when our flight crew referred to each other by first name. Did you just call him Rob? It turns out this is normal in Air Force medical circles, especially on tight-knit flight crews. Okay—cool.

As nervous and absolutely gutted as I was about Sam's condition, I was thrilled to be leaving Landstuhl. We loaded him up on an ambulance bus and drove about ten minutes to Ramstein Air Base to board a C-17 cargo plane.

The plane was a massive gray tube with olive-drab accessories configured to suit the needs of the patients being flown home and their attendants. Instead of a finished floor and uniform rows of seats like a commercial airliner, the C-17 had canvas jump seats lining the sides of the plane. About six feet in from those was scaffolding holding three tiers of canvas cots. In the center, between the rows of stretchers, were more jump seats, but these were shaped like the letter "A," creating a row of seats on either side. The inside of the plane was cold, but the closer you got to the rear of the plane, the colder it was. And that's where they had the unconscious guys like Sam. The wounded troops who were conscious and needed less attention than Sam were stationed closer to the cockpit, where it was more comfortable, along with the other two or three severely injured troops. I sat in the A-frame jump seat across from Sam's cot. It was freezing, but I needed to be as close to him as possible. Seeing his vital signs on the monitor was comforting, though I was both worried and curious about what his intracranial pressure (ICP), measured by the bolt in his head, would do at 30,000 feet for an eight-hour flight.

Other than watching his vital signs, I couldn't do much with Sam. He was in a coma, after all. Talk about dead asleep. Our flight crew took great care of him, which allowed me to relax some, and to my surprise, they took amazing care of me as well. They encouraged me to sleep. Tammy, the RT, set up a warm little bed for me on the floor with her bed roll and several blankets. Even though it was cold, she got me tucked in warm and comfortable. For some reason, tender moments of care and compassion for me like this always made me cry. They still do. When I wasn't asleep, I thought about my life. Whether Sam lived or died, my life was changed forever. I knew I was going to be a young widow, and here I was, only twenty-three. *Maybe I should join the Air Force and do what our flight crew was doing.* I don't enjoy flying, but I guess you get used to it, I mused. After growing up watching *ER*, I'd always been interested in the medical field, and if I were ever to join the military, it would be the Air Force. Hmm... I could be an RT, like Tammy, and then I'd have a great career in the civilian world when I got out. Maybe I'd meet someone in the Air Force and fall in...NO! I can't think like that! Sam's going to be fine. I don't know what our life is going to be like, but it'll be together.

Fortunately, the flight was uneventful. Sam remained stable, and his ICP only increased slightly at altitude. Sam and I touched down at Andrews Air Force Base in Prince George's County, Maryland, just southeast of Washington D.C., on the Sunday afternoon following his injury. Donny was flying back commercial from Germany, and the rest of our family would fly in from Northern California to meet us at the hospital. A liaison from the Army greeted me at Andrews. Wow! This was truly a joint-branch effort. The crew made ready for our fourteen-mile journey to Bethesda Naval Hospital.

The National Naval Medical Center, which many commonly referred to then as Bethesda Naval, is now known as Walter Reed National Military Medical Center and is where troops injured overseas start their medical treatment in the States.

We transferred to a large ambulance bus that accommodated all manner of conditions, including those who were supine on stretchers like Sam, a few in wheelchairs, and several who could walk (aka "walkie-talkies"). Although it was Sunday, the traffic was terrible on the D.C. area roads. Despite our lights and sirens, it was a slow crawl to first drop off several injured troops at Walter Reed Army Hospital before we and several more Marines were taken to Bethesda Naval.

En route, one of the guys on a stretcher (we'll call him Taylor), who was previously unconscious, emerged from his coma as if he was still on the battlefield. His stirring progressed to moaning, which escalated to reaching out and calling for his buddy, we'll call him Gomez. Taylor's calls were gut-wrenching. First, he was searching for Gomez, then apologizing to Gomez.

As our Air Force medical crew came to his aid, he started asking them if they got Gomez. I could hardly watch, but as we were only a couple of yards apart, I couldn't turn away or escape to give him privacy. My heart was in my throat, tears brimming in my eyes. He was in utter turmoil: having been knocked into a coma in Iraq and now waking on a bus stuck in Washington D.C. traffic, all he cared about was the safety of his buddy. My heart broke for him, but all I could think was, *What will happen when Sam wakes up?*

Taylor was dropped off at Walter Reed, so I never got to see what became of him or learn of the fate of Gomez. But perhaps for the first time, I understood the violent reality of war and what it does to the young men and women sent to fight.

Witnessing this heartbreaking scene brought to the surface my greatest fear for Sam, save his death. As tremendous as my fears for his physical survival were, my fear for his mental and emotional stability was even greater. The rate of veteran suicide was rising, and at that time, it was an astonishing twenty-two a day. How could I keep Sam from becoming one of them?

Until I'd heard from the doctor in Germany, his mental and emotional health were my primary long-term worries. He already suffered from PTSD, and now he'd lost four of his guys and endured a fiercely traumatic experience. Knowing Sam, I knew his survivor's guilt would be enough to cripple him emotionally. He was a leader, and Robert Lynch, one of his Marines, had died on his watch. Sam was in no way to blame, but I easily imagined him not being able to see it that way.

It kills me to think about the guys who lived through the blast that killed four young men and injured Sam. It was one of the worst days of their lives, too, and I know they relive it regularly. For this reason, and not wanting to relive it over and over myself, I've never asked any of them for a detailed account of what happened that day in July 2007. I've heard enough details, but I don't want the whole vivid picture.

It would turn out that Sam's cognitive deficits, mostly related to memory, would be a great blessing, largely saving him from the emotional turmoil I predicted. Years later, as I helped orient him to his situation, he would occasionally ask about who else got hurt, so I told him about his fallen comrades. He would be quiet, contemplative, and sad, but the blessing of his memory loss meant that the pain was brief. He'd soon return to the world in the present. Truly, ignorance is bliss.

## BETHESDA'S THIRD FLOOR

The ICU of The National Naval Medical Center in Bethesda, Maryland, made me feel like I was in a dungeon at the bottom of an abyss during a thunderstorm. Even though it was located on the third floor of the hospital, sunlight was obstructed by the building across a courtyard. That accentuated the depressing, sometimes hopeless, and often claustrophobic feeling of having your loved one trapped in a coma, with tubes and machines serpentining his once-magnificent body.

As is the case in most ICUs (and I've had the misfortune of experiencing several), there was a limit of two visitors at a time at Bethesda. If we were very quiet and had a more lenient nurse, we could sometimes sneak three or four of us in at once. The rest of the family waited in the ICU waiting room just across from the always-locked ICU doors that opened only by permission granted by a benevolent nurse on the other side of a wall-mounted intercom. Day after day, we spent our time in this dank waiting room, surrounded by aged "hospital white" walls and "cheerful" hospital art, putting together jigsaw puzzles in companionable silence to avoid voicing our deepest fears.

We came to know the other families in the waiting room, and through their conversations with one another, we could ascertain the condition of their Marine. As much as I would love to say that I celebrated their victories with them, I am ashamed to admit I was jealous.

To me, they didn't know real fear, real uncertainty, real grief. Who cares if he lost a limb? If he's conscious, I have no sympathy for you. Fortunately, this charming attitude did not persist and was probably a manifestation of my anger in the grieving process.

I remember one instance in particular where a wife was describing recent improvements in her husband's condition to her family. I know now that these were signs of emerging consciousness, and in fact, her husband had a very serious traumatic brain injury. But at the time, I didn't even want to listen. She was talking about moving limbs on command and turning his head. Our biggest victory with Sam at that point was minimal pupil dilation in response to bright light and coughing when being deeply suctioned through his ventilator.

Fear and grief can turn you into the worst version of yourself, and someone you don't even recognize looks back at you in the mirror.

CHAPTER EIGHT

# GRIEF AND RECOVERY

Grief or deep sorrow is typically caused by great loss. Sam was still alive, but I had lost a lot. Most of all, I had lost my future—the dream of what my future would be and who I'd spend it with. Not only was I grieving the loss of the man I loved, but the loss of our dreams of drinking lemonade on the porch watching our grandkids play. Now I just prayed he would survive until tomorrow.

I was in shock, a constant state of disbelief and horror.

Though the vision changed over time, the future looked more like an endless reflection of mirrors than a clear vision of what my future, our future, could hold.

But then, life shook me back to reality. Briiing-briiing…briiing-briiing!!!

"Hello."

"Mrs. Nichols? Your husband has taken a turn for the worse. You need to get up here now."

Panic.

Absolute dread.

My abdomen felt like it'd just been hit with a cannonball. I couldn't breathe. Since we were staying in the Navy Lodge on the Bethesda Naval base, I grabbed my phone and called Sam's parents and brother in their rooms so we could make the five-minute walk to the hospital together. It was still dark, but the August air in Maryland was already hot and humid. We raced to the hospital—no one said a word. How does one function with a cannonball-sized hole in their abdomen? I was praying silently, unable to truly form coherent thoughts. Sam's family was probably doing the same thing. No visitor restrictions this time; we were all let in immediately to the ICU. Monitors blared as we approached Sam's room. A flurry of activity surrounded him. I could see by the monitors that his heart rate was in the 220s, and his blood pressure had tanked.

We must have had a conversation with the doctors and nurses, but I have no memory of it. I only saw Sam, and I had an eerie sense of calm and control. Standing on his left side, my back to the crowd behind us, I held his hand and talked to him calmly and soothingly, just as I'd done on so many evenings after his first deployment when PTSD fried his nerves. I stroked his face, held his hand, and smoothed his arm hair, just like I always did.

Perhaps it was because I didn't understand how dire the situation was at the time, but I wasn't pretending to be calm. The crowd that had formed behind us, including our Marine Liaison in his PT shorts and skivvy shirt and the hospital chaplain, were nothing to me.

It was just Sam and me, and he was calming down. I wasn't even crying. One by one, the monitors stopped their alarm signals, and his vitals returned to normal. From chaos to calm. I had a true sense that God was with us, literally wrapping his arms around us in a cocoon of peace. Nothing else existed. I was at peace, and soon Sam was, too. No one could explain why it had happened.

That was just the beginning of a very big day.

## PEG LEG

Later that day, the surgical resident came into Sam's dreary ICU room, his dark green scrubs the only source of color. Sam's dad, Eric, and his brother, Greg, were with me. Sam went to the OR every Tuesday and Friday to have his wounds washed out and debrided of dead tissue. Sam's lower right leg was in rough shape, the resident said. He'd lost three inches of his fibula, the smaller lower leg bone, more than half his calf muscle, and had a gaping hole in his shin. He had wound vacs—a special kind of wound dressing—on all his large wounds, which served to bring fresh blood, remove old blood and tissue, and speed up the healing process, so the wound would be smaller and require less invasive measures to eventually close.

But despite these efforts, it wasn't looking good for the leg. From what the surgeons saw on Tuesday, there was too much necrotic tissue to save it, and waiting any longer could allow the necrosis to spread.

Now, we were having an amputation discussion. A below-the-knee (BK) amputation is preferable to an above-the-knee (AK) amputation due to the function of the knee. Being a BK means the possibility of greater function and faster rehab. Leaving the leg any longer meant risking an AK amputation in the future, not to mention the increased risk of sepsis and death.

Sam was still deeply in a coma at this point. His survival was first and foremost on our minds, so the thought of amputation didn't faze me.

Sure, being an amputee would be hard, especially emotionally, but I would have traded all his limbs for his brain. Take the leg; just save my husband. With no trepidation, I signed the consent form for amputation and was ready to move on, but Sam's dad and uncle had other plans.

They believe in the laying on of hands, a practice taught by Jesus and his Apostles in the New Testament. I grew up Catholic, and this was a new concept to me. Even the idea of praying out loud, anything other than corporate prayer like the Our Father or the Apostles' Creed, was completely foreign to me and felt uncomfortable. But I wanted to honor their beliefs and use every healing means available, so all three of us laid a hand on Sam's right leg as Uncle Greg and Eric prayed. They prayed for complete healing and restoration for the leg such that the surgeons couldn't possibly amputate.

This was my first day as a born-again Christian. That very morning, Sam had almost died before the sun rose. I had been told by an old, white-haired neurologist that Sam was brain-dead and I should sign a do-not-resuscitate order (DNR). I had just signed away permission to amputate a leg that may never be used anyway. And now we were praying. I didn't know what to make of it. I had hope. It had been a very long and emotional day, and I wanted to have faith like my father-in-law and Greg but I was kind of just along for the ride. Donny was in his room at the Navy Lodge packing to fly home during all this leg business, so I brought him the news when I got back there. As is our nature, especially when we're together, we made light of it to cope. We imagined all sorts of iterations of a peg leg. Our favorite was a claw foot from an antique bathtub. Thunk...thunk...thunk... We'd need to get him a parrot, though.

The next day, when visiting hours started at 8:00 a.m., I was there, as always. Distracted by donning my gloves, gown, and mask, I forgot to look for the void in the bed and was shocked when I realized Sam still had two feet. I had to double-check with his nurse that he'd already been to the OR. He had. The leg looked too good to take. Was it a miracle? I think so.

As the days went on in Bethesda, I refused to sign a DNR and insisted on life-preserving measures, such as a feeding tube and a trach, rather than letting Sam starve to death or "pulling the plug." The doctors became more and more concerned about me and consulted with a lady from the Red Cross assigned to the ICU, who served as a counselor to the injured troops and their families.

A few days after Sam's 5 a.m. near-death experience, she asked to speak to me. Her office, where she talked to me about false hope, was a dank hole just as gloomy as the ICU she served. She and Sam's care team were concerned that my mantra of "faith overrules fact" was setting me up for heartbreak when Sam either died or remained in a coma. I couldn't believe her! Lady, I thought, if my husband dies, I'm going to be heartbroken whether I had hope or not! Years later, as I helped orient Sam to his injuries and situation (this had to be done frequently), I'd tell him how the doctors didn't think he'd have a meaningful recovery and that I should pull the plug. My favorite Sam response was, "Showed them."

Yeah, he did.

## GRADUATION DAY

After about three weeks in Bethesda Naval's ICU, Sam was stable enough to graduate to the fabled fifth-floor step-down unit where celebrities visited and free gifts flowed. He was slowly emerging from his coma, and his general health had improved. He had a feeding tube and a tracheostomy. Now, the focus was on wound healing, any necessary surgeries, and hopefully... increased wakefulness.

At this point, Sam was reactive to pain, his pupils dilated in response to bright light, and his eyes were slowly starting to track from side to side. The eye-tracking was something I hardly ever noticed, as it was me he would track as I moved about the room.

Other than Sam's improved health, the next best thing about being on the fifth floor was the atmosphere. Gone were the days of living in a dungeon, taking turns with family between being with Sam and being stuck in the awful waiting room. On the fifth floor, there was no asking permission to see my husband or limit on how many of us could love on him at once.

Instead of the small, stuffy ICU waiting room, there was a spacious, open, airy family room with computers, books, and plenty of places to sit and hang out or play board games. Patients who were able could even hang out in this room for a change of scenery. The best part was that Sam had a huge private room with lots of natural light through the unobstructed windows and plenty of space for family.

Then there were the special visitors. Fortunately, we now live in an era where supporting our troops is not only a good thing, it is expected. Celebrities of all sorts would come to show their support, often bearing gifts. We arrived on the fifth floor the day after the San Diego Chargers cheerleaders came to visit, but there were still plenty of donated laptops to go around. I got my first laptop, a Lenovo ThinkPad. We were there, however, to meet Stevie Nicks.

My dad was the only family member there with us at the time. When the social worker asked if we'd like to meet her, I thought my dad was going to have a stroke. Of course, I said yes.

At the time, I had only fleeting knowledge of Stevie Nicks, but Dad was a big fan. Stevie walked in, wearing the oh-so-flattering yellow isolation gown required in Sam's room, and introduced herself by giving my dad and me hugs. I was mildly starstruck, but my dad was twitterpated. She looked on at Sam, who was "awake," but at that point, it didn't mean much. His eyes were open, and if I walked across the room, his eyes would eventually follow. Two things struck me about our visit with Stevie. Number one, she's really short. I'm only 5'1", and even in her Stevie Nicks boots, I was taller than her in my Converse. Secondly, when someone is grieving, your empathy is far more comforting than your sympathy. She was nothing but well-meaning, but the way she fawned on me and told me how sorry she was and pointed out how young we were, the more I was put in a position to comfort her.

# CHAPTER NINE

# NICHOLS IS STILL ALIVE?

Sam was doing great on Bethesda's fifth floor. His chest tubes came out, he had a successful surgery to put pins in his right elbow, and with the help of occupational therapy, he had begun moving the fingers of his right hand. He also had two successful skin grafts to close the gaping wounds on his right shin and right hip.

And his cognitive status was improving. He was better able to follow commands. The difficulty in assessing whether or not Sam could follow commands (a massive indicator of cognition) was that he was so physically injured there wasn't much he could do to demonstrate his understanding.

His left side was paralyzed from the right hemisphere brain injury, and the right side was riddled with injuries of its own. At one point, I joked, "Maybe he can wiggle his ears," and he did! How did I not know he could do that?! I couldn't believe he hadn't busted out that move in the wooing process. Maybe he was fonder of his eyebrow dexterity, moving them independently with great control.

After his elbow surgery, his right arm was kept in a giant sort of yellow foam Lego-looking thing. It held his elbow at the angle the surgeons wanted it for healing and left just his fingers sticking out of the top. Sam had a terrible wound on his backside, and whenever nurses had to change the dressing or a doctor needed to see it, they had to roll him over on his side, which always caused some pain. It seemed one particular female corpsman was always there whenever this happened, so the nurse and I once joked, "Here comes Doc Winslow, Sam. Flip her off." Ever so slightly, he lifted his middle finger. Yes!

He was making great progress, and it seemed very suddenly that his care team decided he was ready for rehab. This gave me only about forty hours to get ready to go, which included packing up all sorts of free stuff and care packages we'd been gifted and getting it to a hospital volunteer to ship home. You can accumulate a lot in seven weeks, and it wasn't all going to fit in my two bags.

The day we left Bethesda for California, the surgical resident who'd been following Sam told me that when he went to the ICU to gather some sort of information or documentation for Sam's transfer, they were astounded. The ICU doc said, "Nichols is still alive?!" "Yeah, man, and he's headed to acute rehab." They truly had no hope for him.

## PALO ALTO

Approximately seven weeks after Sam's injury, we took a second medevac to Travis Air Force Base, about an hour west of home, for coma-stimulation rehab. I don't remember a thing about that flight, only that I was greeted upon arrival by some amazing humans my dad had been in contact with through a blog he ran about Sam.

Knowing the hospital cafeteria would be closed and that I was basically stranded until morning, they brought me Burger King and a bag with snacks, water, soda, and breakfast bars. I was so touched by their kindness, I barely held back the tears. But I knew that once they started, they wouldn't stop because my emotions from all the change and uncertainty were like a pressure cooker constantly building inside of me.

We spent one miserable night in the David Grant U.S. Air Force Medical Center's ICU. Well, miserable for me. Sam was barely out of a coma and slept for most of it, so I can't tell you whether or not he was miserable. Because of the time it takes to fly cross-country and then the one to two hour drive to Palo Alto, we had to stay overnight at Travis AFB.

In Sam's room they had a chair that converted to a bed there for me. But I didn't normally sleep in his room, so I couldn't relax worrying about him. Thankfully, I usually had the sense to get good rest when I could, but this night I had no choice. Even though I didn't know ventilators then like I do now, it seemed like something just wasn't right about his setup, or at least it was different from what I was used to in Bethesda. I was terribly on edge, stuck in this medical limbo where the nursing staff didn't know us, nor would they ever get to know us. It must have been fine, though, because he was fine.

After surviving the long, tedious night, a critical care ambulance came to pick up Sam in the morning. I couldn't ride with him, so instead rode with our new Marine Liaison, Sergeant Judkins. He would come to be like a big brother to me—actually, to both of us. I get choked up just writing about him. Late morning on a beautiful September Bay Area day, we arrived at the Palo Alto VA, just down the road from Stanford University. Sam was admitted to 7D, the polytrauma unit.

The staff was incredibly knowledgeable, friendly, and kind, but moving from one hospital to another was harrowing. I felt out of control of the situation. I never wanted to move. I'd rather keep the comfort of familiarity than venture into the unknown when it came to Sam, but the choice wasn't mine to make. My emotions were like hot magma rising closer and closer to the surface. I had, and would continue to have, a fear that the next group of people to take care of Sam couldn't possibly be as caring and competent as his previous team. Fortunately, this fear always subsided quickly, and my feelings soon turned grateful and affectionate toward the new crew. We were blessed that Sam was always in caring and competent hands. Once again, he had a large private room. Its large window overlooked a beautiful green lawn, the Arastradero Foothills, as well as Fisher House. I would eventually get to stay at Fisher House, beautiful temporary housing for the families of injured troops or vets who traveled for treatment but didn't warrant admission to the hospital. Unfortunately, there was no room in the inn, so for the first week to ten days of our six-month stay, I had to stay in a motel about ten minutes away. My parents drove down to meet us in Palo Alto and to bring me my car. Once Sam was settled in, they helped me settle into the motel in nearby Mountain View. Loving parents are a blessing. Even after all this, my parents still had a two-and-a-half-hour drive home.

The motel room was drab and dingy with an ugly red-print bedspread—motel chic. But it had four walls and a decent TV. I'd be spending most of my days with Sam anyway, so how much did ugly really matter? As my parents gathered their things and we said our goodbyes, I *lost it*. Out of nowhere, my emotional volcano erupted all over my mom's comforting shoulder.

I felt so alone. When I'd been alone before, I'd felt so much more connected to Sam when we were on base. Now, I was a ten-minute drive away instead of a five-minute walk, and I'd gone from the safety and familiarity of military life to being all alone in the civilian world. I was only without a family member for two days the whole time we were in Bethesda. Now, I was about to be completely alone except for day visits from family.

I hate asking for help. It's not even that I resist it; it's more like it doesn't occur to me to ask. But when my mom offered to stay with me for a few days, I couldn't say yes fast enough. Sometimes, you just need your mom, and I have a great one. My grandparents were planning on visiting that weekend so she could easily get a ride home with them. Her offer, her comforting shoulder, and her obvious love for me were just what I needed in that moment.

The transition soon passed, and I survived. Even better, I quickly came to appreciate the freedom of having my car and having more than our dismal food choices on base in Bethesda. BTW, Silicon Valley has some great Vietnamese and Mexican food if you're ever in the area.

Unit 7D quickly felt like home as I bonded with staff, other patients, and their families. Being only two-and-a-half hours away from home, both Sam's family and mine were able to visit frequently. My aunt, uncle, and cousins even came down with my parents and sister for Thanksgiving. On a doctor's suggestion, we went to Marie Callender's. Palo Alto was the start of Sam's rehab. He had a new regimen: Three hours a day of speech, physical, and occupational therapy, plus a massage therapist twice a week and recreational therapy weekly.

His first three months were more about wound healing than anything else. He had a blast wound on his left buttock that meant he couldn't get into a wheelchair and had to stay in a bed made specially for wound healing. That bed reminded me of the inflatable pool at the end of a slip-and-slide. Only instead of water, the pool portion was a breathable sheet over a bed of tiny silicon beads that were constantly blown around by warm air. Both the warm air and the lack of a firm surface to cause pressure sped up wound healing and prevented any pressure sores.

Sam's butt wound was a pretty big deal. The Palo Alto VA is a teaching hospital connected to Stanford, just a mile or two north. Teams of doctors, wound care nurses, and physical therapists would gather in Sam's room to discuss the progress of the wound and possible next treatment steps.

The wound was on his left buttock, meaning that Sam had to be turned over on his right side for them to view it. It was my job to tend to Sam, the person, while his butt was cared for. I'd crouch down and talk to him, explaining what was happening but also trying to get him to focus on me rather than the score of people crowding into his room.

Sometime later, I read Dr. Jill Bolte Taylor's *My Stroke of Insight* and how she mentally shut down in such circumstances after her stroke, withdrawing from an overwhelming situation. I didn't have her words or the science to teach me during our Palo Alto days, but I could see the withdrawal and stress in Sam. I already knew what his PTSD looked like, and having a crowd in a small room was the perfect trigger.

Sam's butt was so important that it even changed policy on 7D. At the time, the unit didn't have its own wound care nurse or team. The adjacent unit, which served patients with spinal cord injuries, had an amazing wound care nurse, affectionately called the "Purple Lady" because of her love of the color. Occasionally, the Purple Lady would consult on Sam's backside, but she had her own full caseload.

As more and more patients like Sam were expected on the polytrauma unit, the Purple Lady trained a team of two rehab RNs and two physical therapists to become the wound-care team of 7D. By the time we returned to Palo Alto a year later, the 7D wound-care team performed wound rounds twice a week, and the Purple Lady was able to stick to her own unit.

## WHO'S NUMBER ONE?

Sam was slowly emerging from his coma. There's very little difference between being officially in a coma and emerging into consciousness. People don't typically just wake up from non-medically-induced comas. It's a gradual process of increasing wakefulness and improved cognition.

Because of his right-side brain injury, the neurological connection between the brain and the left side was damaged, so Sam couldn't move his left side. His right side, though, was the side with the physical injuries, and he developed a tremor in his right arm and index finger. If he wasn't moving one, he was moving the other. When the arm was going, it kind of looked like he was strumming a guitar against his chest. His index finger moved like he was constantly gesturing, "Come here," rubbing his nail against his chest. From then on, his right index fingernail was always buffed to a smooth shine.

We hoped that when he came off the ventilator and had his trach removed, he'd start talking. Disappointingly, the only time I heard his voice was when he coughed. We tried blinks, but he couldn't control them. Our big communication breakthrough came by accident about four months post-injury.

Donny and Brandi came to visit on their way back from Disneyland, where Donny had proposed. They, Sam, and I were hanging out in his room when Sam's right index finger wiggled, straight-bent-straight-bent.

Donny said, "Sam. What number are you?" Sam held out his index finger to indicate the number one. We stared at each other in amazement.

I asked, "Sam. What number is Donny?" He held out two fingers. WHOA! This is cool!

I began asking Sam yes or no questions, like, "Is your name Sam? One finger for yes, two fingers for no." With some patience and the new finger system, he answered multiple questions correctly. Elated, I ran down the hall and grabbed any therapist I could find. Sam's Speech-Language Pathologist (SLP) wasn't around, but Lana, the other SLP was. I told her to come check out Sam's new trick. He was now a communicator!

Though I didn't know it at the time, this was the beginning of my SLP career.

## MORE TIME IN PALO ALTO

Due to Sam's holey butt, he wasn't allowed to sit in a wheelchair, so his various therapists came to his room for treatment. His therapies included frequent assessments of his cognition, a nerve-racking event for me because I always wanted him to perform well. But, damn, it always seemed like he did his best tricks when no one else was around.

When we first arrived in Palo Alto, Sam could move his fingers and hand upon request. His eyes would slowly track from one side of the room to the other, although he didn't track as well from the right side, past midline to the left.

After about three months in Palo Alto, his wound had healed, and he was finally able to get into a wheelchair and leave the room. This meant he could do therapy in the gym, and we could go outside or to the great room together. We were both thrilled, although I suddenly realized I didn't even have clothes for him. He'd never needed anything but a hospital gown until now. I'd never been more excited to make a Target run for clothes. Finally, after five months, his world could expand beyond four walls, and thanks to our California weather, almost any time was a good time to be outside.

I relished hanging out in the fresh air. One of our favorite indoor activities was me reading *Harry Potter* to Sam. But our favorite outdoor pastime was playing fetch with the therapy dog, Coven, a sweet, docile, old black lab with a graying snout. Sam couldn't throw yet, but we were working on him being able to open his hand to release the ball, and he really enjoyed petting Coven.

Little did we know what an impact Coven would have. Sam started speaking during our twelve-month hiatus up the coast. And despite his lack of short-term memory, he shocked us all when we returned to Palo Alto by remembering Coven. I asked him who Coven was, and Sam said, "A puppy dog."

After six months in Palo Alto, it was time for another move. The coma stimulation program Sam was in was only supposed to be three months, but due to his wound and multiple infections stalling progress, he stayed six months.

But his progress was not as much as we would have liked. Using the one finger for "yes" and two fingers for "no" system, Sam could answer yes and no questions accurately, as long as he was oriented to it each time. His visual tracking continued to improve, although he still had considerable deficits in tracking to the left. His trach had been removed, but heartbreakingly, he wasn't talking and had no form of expressive communication. Most importantly, as long as he was physically capable of a task, he could perform it. His buttock wound was completely healed, and he could now push a bike pedal with his right leg and lift his right arm. This meant that he had the receptive language and cognitive ability to hear a command and follow through. It was a start, but there were still miles to go.

But for me, leaving the coma stimulation program felt like being kicked out; that Sam wasn't good enough, wasn't progressing enough to stay. Fortunately, we had Jen, our social worker, and Sergeant Judkins, whose jobs were to make sure both of us were well taken care of, which even meant housing for me.

As comforting as it was to have them on our team, though, the whole lack of control part was reminiscent of our first year in the Marine Corps. I had to constantly remind myself that I could only control myself, not the situation and that no one was actually against us. Even if it didn't feel like it, the decisions being made *for* us were ultimately for Sam's good. When life is so precarious, any change—even change for the ultimate good—is terrifying.

Jen set up a meeting and evaluation with the patient liaison from Kentfield Rehab and Specialty Hospital, a small rehab hospital in Marin County on the other side of the Golden Gate Bridge. Laurie was a nurse herself and was married to Dr. Barchuk, one of the primary rehab doctors at Kentfield. She deemed Sam a great candidate for the hospital and assigned him to be placed in the care of Dr. Doherty, a specialist in TBI and emerging-consciousness patients.

Laurie and Jen also had an answer to my housing issue. Laurie and Dr. Barchuk had a studio apartment above their garage, and as long as both the doctor and the hospital CEO approved, I could live there for a nominal fee.

We were moving yet again. Time for the next hospital. The next adventure.

# KENTFIELD

Sergeant Judkins accompanied us on the trip up the San Francisco peninsula and across the Golden Gate Bridge to Kentfield. I'm so glad he was there because my first impressions of the tiny hospital were bleak. Gone were the bright white walls and roomy expanses of the Palo Alto VA. This place felt more akin to the dungeon-like Bethesda ICU.

Situated right at the base of Mt. Tamalpais, the whole hospital ached for natural light. The hallways were dark, and the ceilings too low. It felt oppressive. My nerves were already shot, and Kentfield did not make a good first impression. Sam didn't even get a private room. Yuck!

The staff, on the other hand, made up for the hospital's lack of aesthetic appeal. From nurses to CNAs, doctors to therapists, and even the kitchen staff—which included a legit chef, these people knew what they were doing. My fear of letting them care for my Sam was quickly assuaged. If only they could do something about the facility (I'm happy to say they have improved it since then).

The entire staff at Kentfield was incredible. It wasn't just what they did for Sam. They took care of me, too. I was only twenty-four, alone, and my whole life was wrapped up in Sam's prognosis and quality of life.

They took me in, literally, and even socialized with me. I had regular lunches in the tiny cafeteria with Dr. Waters and the neuropsychiatrist, and Celine—a seventy-five-year-old spunky French nurse who adopted me. We saw movies together; she took me with her on the ferry to San Francisco to get her hair done and have lunch and shop. Peggy, a respiratory therapist, took me home with her and introduced me to her daughter, who was my age. I went to parties at their house, sampling the infamous Murphy limoncello and sleeping it off a time or two in the guest room.

I formed a very close bond with Betsy, the hospital chaplain, a beautiful, tall, thin redhead from Georgia. Her husband's job as a movie producer had taken them to London in her thirties. But in the throes of homesickness, she turned to Civil War history for comfort and began writing fiction. Her first book, *Hallam's War*, is a Civil War novel that was published while we were there. She was the first author I'd ever met, and especially after reading the book (I loved it), I couldn't imagine ever taking on such a task. (Yet look what I'm doing now.)

Betsy tended to Sam as best she could, praying with him and talking to him, but she spent even more time with me. We had a weekly date in the cafeteria—coffee for me, tea for her. It was usually light-hearted, a break from Sam and a time to think and talk about other things. But when it needed to be, it got heavy.

Doctor Waters was Sam's internal medicine doctor and a great friend to me. Her job was to keep an infection-prone Sam healthy and comfortable. She was an incredible doctor to Sam, but to me, she felt like an auntie who took me under her wing. And when our stint at Kentfield ended, she touched me deeply by taking a lot of time and effort to make us a scrapbook with pictures and messages from all the hospital staff.

I was living a lonely, scary life. Our families visited often, but day in and day out, it was just me at the hospital with Sam. And every night, I went back to my apartment alone. The relationships I had with people like Betsy, Celine, Peggy, and Doctor Waters kept me going. They were at work, but this was my life, and they were lifelines for me. I'm an introvert by nature, but I craved positive social interaction. I'm so grateful for the time and energy they generously gave me, and I tear up thinking about what they still mean to me.

Dr. Doherty, Sam's rehab doctor, was unbelievable. She sat me down at the nurses' station and drew out a diagram of a neuron (nerve cell), making sure I understood how the meds she gave Sam worked by plugging into receptor sites. She gave me articles that she would discuss with me, making sure I understood them and how they may apply to Sam. But she was much more than a kick-ass physiatrist; she was a trailblazer in the area of neuropharmacology for emerging consciousness patients. She even wrote a chapter on the subject for a neurology textbook while we were at Kentfield and graciously shared it with me. When Dr. Doherty encouraged me to study it and google what I didn't understand, I took it to heart so I could better understand Sam's condition and her goals. Given her more advanced and leading-edge knowledge of the meds that could help Sam, Dr. Doherty made changes to optimize his recovery, starting with the initiation of speech. I was astonished and thrilled when, within forty-eight hours of starting the drug, bromocriptine, Sam was mouthing words. But I wasn't great at reading lips yet—a skill I'm now very good at—and Sam didn't have perfect movement of his lips and tongue, so we struggled. But it was worth it! I started by asking him questions I knew the answer to: Who is the boy wizard with a lightning-shaped scar? What's your middle name? Do you love me? It was a great start.

In addition to reading, we spent a good deal of our free time playing MadLibs outside. I'd ask him for a part of speech. Between his emerging speech skills and the use of an alphabet board, we'd painstakingly get through a page to be rewarded with the hilariously nonsensical story.

Like the Palo Alto VA, Kentfield was an acute rehab hospital where Sam had three hours of speech, physical, and occupational therapy five days a week. In our downtime between therapies and nursing needs, we mostly hung out outside. Inside, the hospital was a dreary, claustrophobia-inducing dungeon, but outside, it was beyond gorgeous, surrounded by green foliage from every angle. Whether we were reading, doing MadLibs, or visiting with friends or family, we spent much of our time on the weather-worn wood deck or a cozy shady spot under a trellis at the front entrance. Donny and Brandi even got married on the back deck because Donny wouldn't get married without his best man, Sam.

The plan was to have a simple ceremony on the deck followed by dinner at a local restaurant. When I told our maintenance guy, Rick, about the wedding and asked if he could move the grill out of the way for the ceremony, he went the extra mile. Not only did he move the grill, he cleaned up and hosed down the whole patio. He even moved some potted plants onto the deck for more color.

Donny and Brandi's wedding was immediate family only—parents and siblings. Sam's eldest brother, Marty, performed the ceremony, having been ordained online just for the occasion. It felt perfect to me—Sam being Donny's best man, just enough people for Sam to be comfortable, and outside in the beautiful setting.

The wedding went off as planned, except for a staying-awake problem with Sam. Especially at this point in his recovery, he would have periods where he simply couldn't open his eyes. He was actually awake, wiggling his tremor finger, and able to speak. He just couldn't get his eyes to open. Consequently, the wedding photos are a bit reminiscent of *Weekend at Bernie's*. All of us dressed up and smiling, and Sam was wearing my sunglasses to block his closed eyes, leaning back in his wheelchair to prevent his head from lolling forward.

The story of Sam's brother not wanting to get married without him had gotten around. We could see the admiring faces looking on from inside the glass doors of the hospital's physical therapy gym.

The icing on the cake for a beautiful, simple ceremony was a complete surprise. The hospital chef made homemade chocolate chip and oatmeal cookies, which he personally delivered for us to enjoy on the deck after the ceremony.

We made lots of memories at Kentfield, but Donny and Brandi's wedding was the most special.

## I'M SO SORRY, ERIN.

Several months into our tenure at Kentfield Rehab and Specialty Hospital, Sam was sent to the main hospital yet again for a severe UTI, an unfortunately common occurrence. Marin General Hospital was a quick mile and a half down Sir Francis Drake Blvd. from Kentfield Rehab. The day after Sam's admission to Marin General, I returned to Kentfield to get some of his things, including various splints and of course, our Harry Potter books. I'd started reading the series out loud to him in Palo Alto, and we were finally on book seven.

As I left Sam's room, I stopped to talk with Dr. Duncan, an infectious disease (ID) doctor. Her husband was the ID doc at Marin General, and they filled in for each other at their respective hospitals, so Dr. Duncan knew exactly what was going on with Sam.

Dr. Duncan had a way of looking directly into you. She was so present with you in conversation. I always appreciated that from her, and I now yearn to do the same with everyone. She looked right at me, touched my arm, and said, "I'm so sorry, Erin." I crumpled; I just completely fell apart. Maybe I felt a finality in her words. I fell so completely apart that she took me upstairs to the offices. I just had to let it out. She sat me down on the couch in Dr. Doherty's office and talked with me for a while, but she had patients to get back to. She told me it was Dr. Doherty's day off and I could stay as long as I needed to. With deep gratitude, I sat there with a box of tissues and cried for about an hour.

My sorrow and fear went beyond Sam's current infection. It was the reality that this was *yet another* infection and the real possibility that, eventually, one of these would take him out. Sam had a growing list of superbugs colonizing (doctor-speak for living in him even when there wasn't an active infection) his body, which required more and more powerful antibiotics and more aggressive treatment, which weakened his already fragile immune system. I had never felt so alone, uncertain, and desperate. When all the tears that could fall had fallen, I steeled myself and went back to Sam at Marin General.

# CHAPTER TEN

# BACK AND FORTH BETWEEN ACUTE CARE AND REHAB

We'd been at Kentfield Rehabilitation and Specialty Hospital for about two months before I spent more than twelve hours away from Sam. Kentfield Rehab, in Marin County, was about an hour and a half away from home. Whenever I went home, I'd spend all day with Sam, leave in the afternoon, and return early the next morning, so he never went long without me.

The day before Easter 2009, I was heading home on I-80 East to Sacramento for the holiday and a birthday get-together for a family friend that evening. The sun was setting on the driver's side, doing further damage to the sun spot on my left cheekbone. Even though it was a mild spring evening, I had that baked-through-the-car-window feeling, and my face was on fire.

The feeling continued when I got to the brewery for the birthday party, so much so that my father-in-law and the birthday girl commented on my warmth and flushed face. But I was drinking beer, so my face was naturally flushed, and I didn't think anything of it. I was just happy to be socializing with people not wearing scrubs or lab coats.

It all made sense when I awoke the next day to the worst cold I'd had in years. My head was pounding, my nose a drippy mess, and my throat on fire. I went to the family Easter celebration at a close family friend's house but spent the entire day lying on the couch, in and out of a feverish sleep.

There was no way I was going to be able to drive back to Kentfield to be with Sam, nor should I be anywhere near him with this cold. I stayed with my parents for another night, hoping to feel human enough to make it back to Sam on Monday. But by Monday afternoon, I still had a high fever and started to suspect this was more than a cold. Family members suggested that I had the flu, but when I last had the flu at age seventeen, I was way sicker. My fever topped out at 103.9. This was just a bad cold, I was certain.

On Tuesday, my mom insisted on taking me to urgent care. The rapid flu test that takes five minutes to process showed positive before the doctor even made it down the hallway with the test. Crap! I was worried about being away from Sam and keeping in contact by calling the hospital. But now I realized that I'd come down with a fever within an hour of the last time I'd seen him and immediately called the hospital to let them know of my positive influenza-A test. As a precaution, his doctor immediately put him on Tamiflu, the same med I'd just been prescribed.

Finally, Friday morning, I was well enough to return to Sam. I had just filled up my gas tank when my phone rang. It was the hospital. CRAP.

Sam had a high fever. They were running labs, and they'd know more by the time I made it there in person. Struggling not to speed excessively and fantasizing about driving a monster truck over the crawling traffic on 101 South, I finally made it back to my Sam.

His diagnosis was pancreatitis, not influenza, and we'd have to go back to Marin General to treat him properly. This would be our first of countless stints there. Although we'd only been at Kentfield Rehab for a couple of months, I had quickly come to feel at home and knew Sam was in great hands. The prospect of going to a new hospital under the care of strangers was always heart-wrenching for me. How could these strangers possibly take care of my Sam the way our regular staff did? They didn't know him, and I didn't know them. Soon, of course, the emergency room staff and medical floor staff became familiar and trusted. The first time was always the hardest, not to mention the fear behind whatever it was that put Sam in the hospital in the first place.

Exhausted from being sick and emotional from Sam being sick, I ended up having a panic attack in the ER. When you're so strong for so long, eventually, the volcano just has to erupt. An amazing nurse took me outside and encouraged me to cry it out and then helped me get my breathing back under control. She brought me back inside then made me eat a sandwich and drink some orange juice. Sam was admitted, and we had a gorgeous view from his third-floor room of the strait connecting the San Francisco Bay to the ocean through the peninsula of Marin County. Seeing the rising headlands with their oaks, redwoods, and eucalyptus, along with the rhythmic falling and rising tide in the bay, did wonders to ease my stress.

On day two of this hospitalization, I was sitting on the edge of Sam's bed, facing him, and taking his paralyzed left arm through range-of-motion exercises. It was only a week before that Dr. Doherty had put him on bromocriptine to help initiate his speech. Who knew that a drug normally used to prevent lactation is also used off-label in cases of brain injury to increase cognitive function?

In only a few days, Sam started to move his mouth. His voice was a kind of weak whisper. If I asked him to say something or asked a question I knew the answer to, I could read his lips. Seeing "I love you" on his beautiful lips was more powerful than I can begin to describe—it took my breath away and made my heart soar. So, there I was, sitting on the edge of his bed, working his left arm, when something told me to stand up. The second I did, he threw up. He gurgled, "I barfed," and then looked up at me. "Barf." We have a voice!

Sam had a voice.

I had renewed hope.

And I was about to take a chance and learn a very important message.

## THE ANGRY WIFE

About five months into our stint at Kentfield, the Wounded Warrior Project contacted me about the Brain Injury of America Caregivers' Conference. They were offering me free entry, airfare, and hotel stay at the Dallas/Ft. Worth Westin, where the conference was to be held. All I'd have to pay for was food.

It seemed like a no-brainer, but it was only about thirteen months after Sam's injury. In part, I was afraid to leave him for three or four days. I hadn't been away from him for more than about eighteen hours at this point post-injury, except when I had the flu. My real trepidation, though, were the questions that might be *answered*. I'd learned a lot in just over a year, but there were questions I hadn't asked for fear I'd get an answer I didn't want to hear—that whole ignorance is bliss cliché. In the end,

I decided this was an opportunity I shouldn't pass up. I could always retreat to my room and watch TV if stuff got too real. Lee Woodruff, wife of the journalist Bob Woodruff, was the keynote speaker. Although she spoke to a mostly civilian audience, and her husband was a civilian himself, Bob was treated at Bethesda Naval Hospital after being hit by an IED in Iraq, just like Sam. The familiarity of her experience in the dreary third-floor ICU and her elation at Bob's graduation to the fifth floor comforted me. I felt like she was speaking directly to me.

Like my experience with Lee's keynote, I was happily surprised to be comforted by the ease with which I could talk to the other caregivers in attendance because I didn't have to give a science lesson in order to talk about Sam. Unlike talking to my family and friends, they understood the ins and outs of TBI rehab and medical issues. Talking to these other caregivers actually felt relaxing and cathartic rather than exhausting, like most conversations about Sam had become.

Except for one conversation. The solitary military wife I met was very angry. We talked in the open corridor outside the main ballroom, sharing about our husband's injuries. I don't remember anything about her husband other than feeling sorry for him because his wife had such a bad attitude. She was angry about the Iraqis who did this to her husband. She wanted to go over there herself and get her revenge. Whether she spoke of the Army or medical personnel, this woman had nothing positive to say. Talking to her was exhausting.

But she left a profound impression on me. I didn't want anyone—especially Sam—to feel the way I felt talking to Mrs. Angry Pants. I recognize that we all grieve at our own pace and in our own way—clearly, her way was not my way.

I could acknowledge the suck. It sucked that Sam was blown up and had a severe TBI. It sucks that three Marines and a Navy Corpsman died, and their families are in mourning. It sucks that our dreams for our future will never come true. It sucks that I'll probably never have a sex life again. It sucks that I never have someone to take out the trash, pump my gas, or surprise me with Jamba Juice anymore. What doesn't have to suck is my attitude. I have a choice. We all do.

Being a young military wife taught me to control the controllable. I couldn't control Sam's orders or the decisions of his commanders nor the United States' involvement in Iraq. I could, however, control the way we spent our time together.

I wanted Sam to want to come home to a supportive wife who didn't make the situation harder because of her attitude. This didn't mean I agreed with every decision that affected us or that I didn't show emotion when things didn't go the way we wanted. Early on, I threw a remote control and punched a wall. I threw fits. And guess what? It got me nowhere. It also left Sam in a position of having to deal with me on top of having to live with the situation itself. I quickly learned how unhelpful my angry or frustrated attitude could be.

My time as a military wife trained me to have an attitude that set us up to thrive in any situation. It's not being a doormat; it's simply accepting what you can't control and focusing on what you can control so you and everyone around you aren't miserable. I could control the way I spoke to the staff. A nurse in Bethesda once told me the staff loved coming into Sam's room. Despite the bleak circumstances, it was a positive place to be. I was respectful, kind, and engaging, which made them serve with even greater hearts, which benefited Sam. What benefited Sam benefited me.

In *Man's Search for Meaning*, Viktor Frankl says, "Everything can be taken from a man but one thing: the last of the human freedoms—to choose one's attitude in any given set of circumstances, to choose one's own way." My way was to be as positive and grateful as possible. I could be in pain, but I didn't have to suffer.

## MY READING INSIGHTS

After I took the chance to go to the Brain Injury of America Caregiver's Conference, I was ready to learn more. Dr. Doherty had been teaching me little bits. Now I wanted books. I picked up a copy of *Netter's Concise Neuroanatomy* and a book I'd heard about at the conference, *The Brain that Changes Itself*, by Norman Doidge, a collection of clinical examples of neuroplasticity—the brain's ability to change itself.

Due to his right hemisphere brain injury, Sam couldn't move the left side of his body. So, after reading a story on phantom limb pain, I wanted to see if Sam and I could get the same neuroplastic effect for volitional movement as for decreasing pain. In the case of phantom limb pain, patients put their hand in a mirror box and performed motor tasks like opening and closing the hand. The brain perceived the right hand in the box as the mirror image, or the left hand. This "rewired" the brain's sensory networks. The patient could move what appeared to be the missing left hand without pain. Over time, using the box, the phantom limb pain went away.

My hypothesis was that we could do the same rewiring in the motor cortex as the phantom limb case did in the sensory cortex. So I built my prototype mirror box out of a balsa wood set, crazy glue, and small mirrors from Michael's. Later, my grandpa built a much larger box more suited for a man's hands.

I wish I could say the experiment worked, but the truth is, I didn't work with Sam and the box often enough to see any results or present any scientific findings. The problem was that it was hard to place Sam's hands in the box and have the mirrors at the right angle for him to see the reflection. But reading, researching, and taking action to help Sam was a good first start. I couldn't control the situation, but I could control how I responded.

Sometime after I created the box prototype, Dr. Doherty told me about a brain researcher who had a stroke and wrote a memoir about her experience and her recovery. The next day, she burst into Sam's room. "Quick! Turn on Oprah!" There was Dr. Jill Bolte Taylor promoting her book, *My Stroke of Insight.*

I immediately went out and bought the book and began applying her insights to Sam. Dr. Bolte Taylor's list of "things I needed" helped shape the way I interacted with Sam. It was the catalyst for a presentation I would later craft, "Service Delivery to Veterans with TBI: a Caregiver's Perspective." Most of all, though, the book helped me recognize what Sam needed to thrive. It helped me understand the perils of neural fatigue, of shutting down when overwhelmed, and the value of even small bits of control—like having the lights on or off. There is a direct link between my decision to take action rather than being a victim of our circumstances and Sam's quality of life. Sam's improved communication and quality of life had a direct impact on our relationship and my own quality of life.

Between Dr. Doherty's tutelage, Dr. Doidge's and Dr. Bolte-Taylor's books, I became a student of TBI and, most impactfully, an expert on Sam. As the years went on, my knowledge and expertise continued to expand, and I became a licensed Speech-Language Pathologist.

## NIGHTS

Nights were the worst. Nights are where hope and positivity fail to conquer dark thoughts. When Sam was deployed, I was really good about not thinking about the danger, the loneliness, the possibilities.

But some nights—lying in bed alone, praying for his safety, and feeling so very, very far away from him—it was all I could think of.

Within six months or so of Sam's injury, our reality had set in and become the new normal. I no longer woke with the one and a half seconds of bliss before my heart sank in despair and my chest had the too-familiar sensation of being crushed. In a few months, I woke like it was any other day and got ready to see my husband through a day of therapies and whatever medical drama the day held.

In the dark of night and the loneliness of my bed no longer empty for the course of a deployment, but indefinitely, my stomach turned to knots, and rogue thoughts of "why me" and "how is this my life" ran rampant through my head, unguarded by my daytime defenses and distractions.

I'm writing this at night. I'm not a night owl, but tonight, I couldn't sleep. There's a pain in my gut I know to be grief. With time and therapy, I've learned to distinguish the difference between depression, which feels like nothing; anxiety, which feels like vibrating out of my body; and grief, which feels like a fist twisting just behind my belly button and stealing my air.

Nights are when most of the phone calls came. I have a note on my phone from 2019:

"This is one of those nights, and there have been many others when I decide to shower and wash my hair before I go to bed rather than risk getting a call overnight and not being able to shower in the morning. Also, I should always get gas on the way home when I am running low in case I get a call in the middle of the night. It's always the middle of the night."

One time, I had a terrible cold, so I stayed home instead of spending the day with Sam. I'd just taken some NyQuil around 9:00 p.m., and within seconds of swallowing it, the phone rang. For some reason, that time, I met Sam at his rehab home instead of going straight to the hospital.

The nurse and I stepped into the hallway while the now-familiar paramedics from the fire station around the corner transferred a feverish Sam from his bed to their gurney. Exhausted and sick, I leaned against the linen closet door next to Sam's room and slid to a low squat.

When they were ready to roll Sam out to the ambulance, I stood up to get out of the way. But the NyQuil had dropped my blood pressure, and luckily, the nurse caught me as I nearly passed out from the position change. Whew, fighting my cold, sedation, and advocating for Sam made that an extremely long night in the ER.

As a health coach, I can teach you all about sleep hygiene and your circadian rhythm. But too much blue light isn't what's keeping me up tonight. It's the clenched fist behind my belly button and the tears that just won't stop.

## MORE KENTFIELD

Plagued by recurrent infections and a bout of pancreatitis, Sam managed to stretch out our three-month stint at Kentfield to twelve months. By the time he was discharged, he could talk some (with varying degrees of intelligibility), hold his head up with no support for brief periods of time, and had greatly improved his core strength in sitting at the edge of the mat table. He still had no short-term memory, and his long-term memory was on a kind of sliding scale. He often thought we were about sixteen, but giving him a timeline of events would usually jog his memory to the times before his injury.

During our time at Kentfield, I discovered what I wanted to be when I grew up. I'd always been interested in physical therapy, having had shoulder surgery at fifteen and re-injuring my shoulder after going from doing almost no exercise for eighteen months to doing P90X in my studio apartment over the Barchuk's garage. The next day, I woke with a familiar feeling in my shoulder and a sinking feeling in my gut. At Kentfield, with Sam in physical therapy, I realized I love the field of rehab. But it didn't seem prudent to put all my educational eggs in an injury-prone basket. So what about speech? Sam's incredible Speech-Language Pathologist, Linda, was already teaching me about him and how to work with him. When I told her I was interested in Speech-Language Pathology, she took every opportunity she could to teach me something. At one point, she even asked me to speak about my perspective as a caregiver to a class she taught at San Francisco State University. This personal experience put me far ahead once I entered speech school.

After a year in Kentfield, it was time to move yet again. We'd be heading back to our hometown area soon to a small sub-acute rehab home, but not before another short stint at the Palo Alto VA to make sure they had done all they could for Sam.

## CARE MERIDIAN

After an uneventful two months back at the Palo Alto, VA, we headed home to Care Meridian, a rehabilitation home in Granite Bay, about three miles from Folsom Lake, where we were married. When Sam was admitted in mid-May 2009, it was a three-bedroom, six-bed facility on a beautiful rural property. The neighbors were farmers and ranchers, but it was still close to the luxuries and conveniences of suburbia. Best of all, it felt like a home. It had a large great room with an interior built of knotty pine and a huge brick fireplace on one wall. It was not my first aesthetic choice, but its homey charm was unparalleled.

Perhaps the greatest feature of Care Meridian, besides its staff, is the property it sits on. The front and side yards feature a beautiful green lawn, granite rocks, oak, and pine trees, as well as towering palm trees you can see from the main road a third of a mile away. We had a view of neighboring pastures and their free-range livestock. And one time, we even came home to find an escaped cow grazing on the front lawn.

Care Meridian was "home" for nearly eleven years, from May 2009 until April 2020. During that time, it became a larger, fifteen-bed facility, with eleven of those fifteen beds being private rooms. The knotty pine and brick fireplace are gone, replaced with your standard up-to-code drywall and contemporary decor of tans and blues, but the homey vibes and focus on family, activities, and shared space remain. Sam's first private room was decorated with his stuff, including the Pee Wee Herman doll that hung from a hook in his ceiling, just like he had it as a teenager and which I'd gazed at as I wrote him my daily letters during his first deployment. After the remodel, Sam was the most senior patient, so we got the first choice of the new rooms and chose a corner room with two windows overlooking the backyard with its beautiful pond.

There was very little staff turnover at Care Meridian, which enhanced the continuity of care. But most of all, it allowed us to form great relationships with staff. It may sound trite, but it was a family. I knew that when I wasn't there, they took care of Sam like they'd take care of their son or brother. Despite his lack of memory, the familiarity of the staff helped with his level of comfort and, therefore, his compliance.

We had family events there, including a big party for our fifteenth wedding anniversary. I partially raised my nieces and nephew there. All three of them spent time at Care Meridian, from the baby carrier and port-a-crib to running around playing balloon volleyball with Uncle Sam, jamming with us in music therapy, or crushing whiffle balls in the backyard. For about two years, I watched my oldest niece three days a week. She was with me all day at Uncle Sam's, and I even kept a port-a-crib in Sam's closet and stored her Elmo DVDs with his own collection.

Most of all, it was my home base. Finally, we had a place to call home–a place where I could stretch out on the couch and watch TV, holding hands with Sam in his wheelchair, or move the living room furniture to set up a movie day with Sam, the kids, and even other patients.

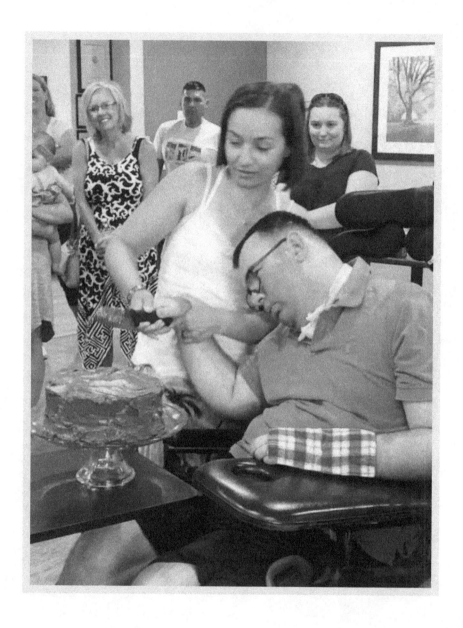

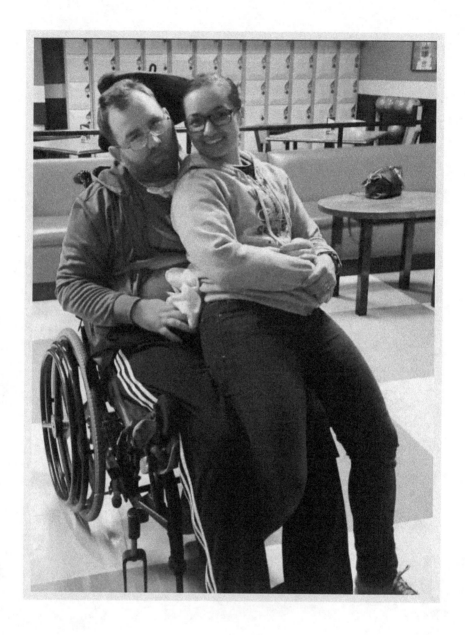

# CHAPTER ELEVEN

# SAM'S NEW NORMAL

We had reached the point in Sam's journey where most of his progress had been made. He continued to make improvements over the next many years, but by and large, within two years of his injury, we had a good idea of who Sam was and what he was capable of.

He knew who I was and who our family was. He had basic knowledge that anyone would have from growing up with an American high school education. His biggest cognitive deficit was his lack of short-term memory. He had no ability to track time and usually thought we were still teenagers. Because of this, he asked me to be his girlfriend on the regular and proposed marriage more times than I could count. I might ask him if he wanted to go outside and read, and he'd say he couldn't because he had to go to class or he had to ask his mom. Fortunately, we never repeated our breakup or dysfunctional teenage behavior.

One time, we were sitting in the knotty-pine-clad great room when he said, "Nernie, you want to be my girlfriend?" I tapped our wedding rings together. "Well, I'd love to, but we're already married."

He stared at me, stone-faced. "What?" But his expression said, "This chick is nuts."

To give you an idea of Sam's cognitive status, one day we were watching TV in his room. When a commercial for a Gillette razor with a pivoting head came on, he told me, "I *need* that maneuverability." I couldn't understand "maneuverability," but he was able to spell it for me. He had always been a great speller, and his TBI didn't change that. His therapists often asked him how to spell a word as they wrote progress notes, including the often mispronounced "lackadaisical."

Sam could have been a writer. Before his injury, he had incredible language skills and an IQ of over 150. In high school and his first year of college, he excelled in creative writing—especially with scripts.

In our junior year at our high school, we had a big project called "Decades." You were put into groups that got scored in both history and English classes, and each group had to cover the major events of an entire decade during an entertaining presentation. Sam's group got the 1960s, so he wrote, produced, directed, and starred in a gritty Vietnam War short film.

Then, we had to complete a senior project in order to graduate. It involved having a mentor, putting in a certain number of hours of work, and presenting a final product—like a guitar you built or performing a piece you learned on the guitar, for example.

Sam wrote a comic book illustrated by his brother. Though it was a collaboration between them, Sam had ultimate creative control and produced an impressive, one-shot graphic story.

Cleaning out some old boxes last year, I discovered Sam's zombie Western in a beat-up, Iraq-dust-encrusted black-and-white composition book. He loved zombie movies (long before *The Walking Dead* made them popular). He was also a huge Samurai movie fan, and *The Magnificent Seven* is a remake of the Japanese classic *Seven Samurai*, Sam's favorite movie.

Here's Sam's first paragraph (as well as I can decipher from his atrocious handwriting):

> *A thin sliver of light spilled from the hilltop, illuminating the vivid landscape of the dead and dying valley. Sunrise on Valle le Gusta is a sultry and sensuous dance of life and virility in a serene environment inhabited only by what God put there. A wisp of wind carries dandelions adrift, carefree; desert blossoms shy until the cool spring breeze beckons to them, peek out their delicate little heads to greet the new sun. Insects begin to flutter about in patterns, exploring and feeding on the life-giving/nurturing _____ of the western frontier.*
>
> *But not today.*

I really want to know where his story was going. I so badly wish he was co-writing this memoir with me. His descriptions were far better than mine will ever be. The irony is, without his injury and the road it put us on, I wouldn't have this story to write. It's hard to imagine a story that doesn't include trauma, fear, heartache, wheelchairs, cuddling in hospital beds, blood draws, IVs and catheters, and ongoing therapy—our version of normal.

Sam was pretty content as long as he was comfortable and mildly entertained. His right hemisphere brain injury actually made him oblivious to his injuries and level of deficit, which was really a blessing. It's called anosognosia and is common for people who have experienced trauma to the right hemisphere. Even sitting in a wheelchair, he'd tell you he didn't need it—that he could walk. He once tried to arm wrestle me with his paralyzed left arm. When nothing happened, he said, "It's too easy." To my great relief and immense gratitude, he could live in the moment and not dwell on his struggles.

He had a great quality of life, and we were able to continue being best friends as well as husband and wife. Sam had always been very fond of my butt, and the lack of filter now from his TBI made that quite clear. Whenever I stood next to him, he put his right arm around me, and that hand would grab what he wanted, regardless of who was watching.

One time, we were in the radiology waiting room at the VA. His hand was all over my butt, and when I reminded him we were in public, he said he didn't care. It was only when I appealed to his jealous side and pointed out that his touching my butt drew other people's attention to it that he finally relinquished his grip. Much of Sam's personality stayed intact after his injury—especially his thoughtful side. One morning around 10:00 a.m. at Care Meridian, I walked into Sam's room to find his CNA, Andy, finishing up Sam's morning hygiene and getting him ready for the day. Andy was combing Sam's hair when Sam asked me (serious as could be), "Babe, do you have any cash?"

"No. Why?"

"To tip him," Sam answered, gesturing with his head back towards Andy.

Andy and I looked at each other, both trying not to laugh and our hearts swelling. I explained to Sam that Andy is his CNA, not his barber.

"All I need, Bud," Andy said, "is a tip of the cap."

Sam looked up at me and said, "Get me a hat."

I grabbed an Indiana Jones-style hat from a push pin on the wall and handed it to him. He clumsily put it on his head and, looking right at Andy, tipped his cap.

What strikes me as so endearing about that moment and others like this one is just how "normal" Sam seemed—if it weren't for him having the context so wrong. Because of his short-term memory loss, he wasn't oriented to time or place and used context clues to figure out his location.

This tip of the cap is the perfect example of how Sam was still Sam. He'd been chivalrous and extremely charming and polite ever since I'd known him as a boy about to turn fourteen. He'd practically knock me over to open a door for me, and even though his ability was limited, he still always did what he could to be a gentleman.

Whenever I'd tell him I was going out to grab lunch, he'd ask if I needed money, struggling to get his hand into his front pocket. When I told him about a run or a bike ride my friends and I were doing, he'd ask if we needed a ride.

Moments like these made the late nights and long days in the hospital, the worry, the stress, and the loneliness at home more than worth it. Sam's worthiness was never a question. My marriage certainly wasn't what I'd expected, but my husband was amazing, and I'd do anything to make him feel loved, happy, and safe. He was doing it for me all the time.

Our circumstance was certainly nothing I'd ask for, but I've never known another woman who can say with the same degree of certainty that her husband loved her more than anything. Sam cherished me, and it was clear for all to see.

Unfortunately, Sam's chivalry wasn't the only thing that carried over from our pre-injury life. PTSD continued to be a part of our reality. And the event that caused his greatest anxiety was the annual Care Meridian Christmas party. All of the staff, patients, and patients' families celebrating together in the great room could make him sweat. Many a time in our eleven Christmas parties there, Sam and I made an early exit. His tremor was always present if he was awake, but it gained a ferocity when he was stressed. I'd often take him back to his room and split my time between hanging out with him and enjoying the food and fun.

And I still have my own PTSD. To this day, I hate the sound of phones ringing because I've been woken countless times by the phone and an emergency on the other end. I guess you could say it's a trigger. Phones ringing, especially the "old school phone" ringtone on iPhones, are my nails on a chalkboard. Years ago, I had to change my ringtone to stop the inevitable moment of panic that came every time I got a call. My ringtone is now a song from Moana, which doesn't send me into hyper-vigilant mode. I can't change other people's ringtones, though, so I'm often reminded of my middle-of-the-night emergency panic when I'm in public.

Sam's buddies are also terribly afflicted with PTSD. We've lost a few, including a good friend from high school who served as an Air Force Special Policeman and deployed three times. It tears me up to think about what they've seen and that they relive the trauma over and over.

# CHAPTER TWELVE

# LIFE BEYOND REHAB

About two years into TBI life, I threw out my back—again. I'd sprained it working as a server at the country club when I was seventeen, and it had a bad habit of going into spasms a few times a year.

Sam and I had been blessed with a loaner wheelchair van, but the process of getting him in and secured was quite physical. I was only twenty-five, but there I was with my back in spasms again. I couldn't keep going this way, I thought. Sam needs me to be fit and able-bodied, and I need to be healthy for me. It was time for a change. I needed a day for me.

For over two years, I'd been with Sam every day, except for a few days when I had the flu. Dr. Doherty used to tell me that part of Sam's rehab was communicating with other people besides me, which could only happen when I wasn't there. He was in a great rehab home with amazing care and attention, so I told our family I'd no longer be at Sam's on Saturdays. If they didn't want him to be alone, that'd be a great time for them to visit him.

My only obligation on Saturdays was to go to the gym. I'd get there mid-morning, hit the elliptical to warm up, then run for a mile and finish with a weight circuit. I kind of knew what I was doing, but I didn't have any clear goals at the time other than to get moving. I also knew I needed a strong core to protect my back and that Pilates had something to do with the core. Eventually, I got the nerve to join a Pilates class. Have you ever had one of those "this is the first day of the rest of your life" moments? That's what my first Pilates class was like. It was challenging, but I'm always up for a challenge, especially when it's physical. The real life-changer, though, was the instructor.

After a couple of months of taking her class, Suzanne and I started talking about cycling. I'd recently bought my first road bike in order to rehab a knee injury I got from trying to turn myself into a runner overnight. We went on our first ride together the following Saturday after class, and our friendship, as well as my career as an endurance athlete, was born.

Suzanne is eight and a half years older than me and has been the big sister I've needed these past eleven years. She helped build my confidence in running and cycling; she somehow even got me into the water and turned me into a triathlete. Our hours on the bikes together, running the trails, and traveling to the Bay Area for fun adventures were my therapy. I can't imagine where I would have been emotionally if I didn't have the physical outlet of training but also the long conversations we had about life and faith.

Aside from the friendship, training gave me something I could control. I couldn't control the health and safety of Sam. I couldn't control the biggest factor that determined my life circumstances, but I could show up to the gym, to the trail, to the race. I could put the work in and get results. If I slacked off, my performance suffered. If I worked hard, slept well, and fed myself well, I performed well. I had that control.

Whether you're training for races, competing in bodybuilding or CrossFit, or just working out for yourself, physical training is the greatest teacher of reaping what you sow. It's also the greatest tool for sharpening your ability to deal with hard things.

When you choose to do hard things—like getting up early on a Saturday morning to run or hitting the gym after work, grinding out a run that sucks, or pushing past the desire to bail out early on your workout and finish strong—you are training for life. Life is hard. I got 3:00 a.m. phone calls to meet Sam in the emergency room. Time and time again, I had to make life-and-death decisions on little sleep. I believe that my physical training prepared me to keep dealing with the stress of these life moments, no matter what.

## BACK TO SCHOOL

In the Fall of 2009, a little more than two years after Sam's injury, I went back to school and started slow. I had fifty units already and needed ten more to transfer to Sac State (California State University, Sacramento, but nobody calls it that) to study Speech-Language Pathology. I needed to take Statistics and Deaf Studies 1 & 2, which needed to be in subsequent semesters.

Taking two classes on my first foray back to school allowed me to wean myself away from Sam just a bit. My community college, Sierra College, was only ten minutes away from Sam's rehab home, and my Statistics class was in the evening after I'd usually leave for the day anyway. Sam was very needy at this time, and leaving him was heartbreaking, but he needed to manage without me sometimes, and I needed to do this for me.

Part of going back to school when I did was because my mind felt like it was turning to mush. Other than engaging with the therapists and nurses, I just hung out with Sam all day, which involved watching a lot of TV and reading for pleasure. Even though I was standing by my husband, which is where I wanted to be, it was hard not having any direction. I needed to be challenged. I needed to take action on some sort of future. I was twenty-five and not ready to live a retired life.

Part of what made it so difficult to leave Sam was his confabulation. Confabulating is when the brain perceives an alternate reality to the truth, and the person 100% believes it's true. There was a patient at Care Meridian, Tony, who had a stroke and was a big confabulator. He'd been a truck driver, and one time told me that he, Sam, and Richard took a haul up to Wyoming the night before... impossible for so many reasons.

Sam's confabulation was different; it almost always had to do with the setting and the people there. His confabulation was usually that he was on a ship, and "these people" (the nursing staff) were criminals. Sometimes he was in prison but innocent and surrounded by criminals. Sometimes, the ship was a spaceship, or he was trapped in a video game. If I got to his room and he asked me how I found him, I knew he was confabulating. I was the only thing that was right and good in this scenario, so leaving him was torture. One time, when I needed to leave for class, Sam clung to my waist with his good right arm. I asked Denise, the most caring and motherly CNA I've ever known, to come help. I explained to Sam that she was a good guy and she'd take care of him. Like a distraught toddler being passed from mom to the babysitter, I had to pass a worried Sam off to Denise, moving his arm from around my waist to hers. My heart was in my gut. I knew he was safe and in good hands, but it killed me to leave, hearing him hollering my name as I walked down the hall. When he wasn't upset with the staff because he thought they were "bad guys," Sam was quick to offer his appreciation.

He had a nurse named Hira, and one time, he told her, "You can be my Hira, baby," purposefully misquoting the Enrique Iglesias Jr. song.

In the fall of 2010, I transferred to Sac State as a Junior, majoring in Speech-Language Pathology and Audiology. It was a difficult major, made more difficult by the knowledge that in order to get into graduate school, I had to basically get straight A's and participate in extracurricular activities like volunteer work, along with anything put on by the department. But there was no choice not to—I had to have my master's degree to be a speech therapist.

That junior year involved all-day school only two days a week. On Mondays, Wednesdays, and Fridays, I got to be with Sam. When he wasn't doing therapy, I'd read my textbooks aloud to him, learn by explaining a concept to him, or work quietly while he watched TV. Juggling Sam, my workouts, and school was hard, but I was busy and more fulfilled than I'd ever been.

I graduated with my bachelor's degree in Speech-Language Pathology and Audiology in the spring of 2012 and began grad school at Sac State that fall. My schedule changed from semester to semester, but I always had a day or half days each week dedicated to Sam. I was with him as often as I could be, and he was always my best study partner/guinea pig.

Learning about normal brain anatomy and the neurobiology of speech, language, cognition, and swallowing helped me understand Sam and his deficits better. Having a real-world example helped me contextualize what I was learning, and the more I learned, the more I could apply it to Sam to improve his quality of life, especially for his communication and orientation.

In fact, his orientation was a big part of his daily routine. I knew through my experiences with Sam and through classes about different types of memory that he could learn new things if they were repeated often. For example, he had a routine with his physical therapist for the process of transferring from his wheelchair to the mat table. He couldn't tell you the steps, but he could do the steps, often knowing what came next without prompting.

I used this feature of his procedural memory to create an orientation script to help decrease the distress of being disoriented. That had the added benefit of reducing his confabulation and increasing his compliance with the nursing staff.

There are only so many ways you can say what happened, so my story usually came out nearly verbatim every time, anyway. I turned what happened to him and where he was into a script where he filled in the blanks. This gave him more ownership of his own story. I even strapped a button to his armrest that played a recording of me saying the script so he could hear it from my voice whenever he needed it. The script went like this:

Erin: You're at your rehab…

Sam: Home.

Erin: In…

Sam: Granite Bay.

Erin: You're at a rehab home because you were hit by a…

Sam: Roadside bomb

Erin: Doing your job as a U.S.

Sam: Marine

Erin: In…

Sam: Iraq.

Erin: The roadside bomb gave you a traumatic…

Sam: Brain injury

Erin: Which gives you really poor short-term…

Sam: Memory.

Erin: So you often forget where you are, why you're here, and what's going on. Your nurses and CNAs are here to help…

Sam: Take care of me.

Erin: And they are your…

Sam: Friends.

Erin: You need to help them…

Sam: Help me.

We added the bit about the nurses and CNAs being his friends because he would sometimes hit their hands away and resist their help because he thought they were "bad guys." The nurses, CNAs, and therapists were able to use this script as well, which helped them with Sam when I wasn't there. It was incredible to be able to take something I learned from school and apply it directly to Sam to improve his life.

My time in college was met with its fair share of challenges, as anyone's is. I had many classmates who were moms, single moms even, and I couldn't imagine how they got all their homework and studying done while taking care of kids. Likewise, no one could imagine my scenario: getting phone calls from doctors and nurses at school, having to send a CNA or therapist with Sam to a doctor's appointment because I had class, or as in one case, almost having to drop out of grad school because of a hospitalization.

In my first year of grad school, Sam came down with severe pneumonia, landing him in the ICU on a ventilator. I didn't care what the ramifications were—if Sam was in the hospital, I was there with him. By maintaining good communication with all my professors and clinical instructors, who all knew about Sam, they always understood when I missed class. And knew that I did my best to keep up with what I could from the hospital.

The pneumonia situation was potentially dire. Someone who's been on as many antibiotics as Sam has a weakened immune system. I knew from my schooling that the breathing tube could remain in his throat for only a ten to fourteen-day window before they'd have to perform a tracheostomy.

He'd had a trach early on, and now that he could talk, I was extremely concerned about his ability to communicate with a trach. I also feared for his safety, worried he'd pull it out. He had a history of pulling out important "medical accessories" because, as he once put it, he "wondered what it did." I was afraid we'd have to keep his one usable limb restrained so he wouldn't cause himself significant harm.

*My* plan for his treatment was to wean him off the vent ASAP to prevent the need for a trach. When I met Dr. Aghilli, one of the several pulmonologists who would care for Sam countless times over the next many years, his first remark to me was, "So, you're the wife who doesn't want a trach?"

"That's me."

I told him my concerns. I reminded him that we were only a few days into the ten to fourteen-day window, and this was a decision that didn't yet need to be made, although I understood the tracheostomy was certainly a possibility.

On the morning of day ten or eleven of Sam being on the vent, I heard from the respiratory therapist that as long as Sam's blood gas (a measurement of various gases like oxygen and carbon dioxide in the blood) came back good, the plan was to extubate (pull out the breathing tube) after rounds.

That was amazing! The only thing was, I had an exam.

I'd planned to go to school at noon for the test, but I definitely couldn't leave before they extubated because I needed to be there to talk to Dr. Aghilli. I needed to be there in case something happened. Even if nothing went wrong, I needed to be with Sam as he was coming out of sedation.

It was only around 8:00 a.m., so I emailed my professor, Dr. Goldsworthy, hoping she'd be able to respond before I had to make the decision to stay with Sam or go to school. She was one of those teachers who got upset if you missed a class. How was she going to respond to me missing an exam? My whole body relaxed when she graciously told me it sounded like I was where I needed to be, and we'd work something out.

Meanwhile, I got an email from our clinic director, Mrs. Oldenburg, that the faculty had discussed my situation, and they'd like me to come into a meeting on Monday (it was mid-week) if I wasn't able to return to classes and clinic next week. Was I being kicked out for too much time missed? Would they let me in with the cohort the semester behind me? I cared, but Sam was what actually mattered, so I tried not to stress over it.

Later that morning, Sam's sedation was discontinued, his vent detached, and he was extubated. Dr. Aghilli told me that the day we met, he didn't think there was a chance of Sam ever coming off the vent, let alone being extubated. That was his first lesson in not underestimating Sam.

I got another email in the early afternoon. It was Dr. Goldsworthy with a huge surprise. (Sorry, Dr. G., I'm going to tell our secret.) She sent me the exam and told me to return it ASAP and not to tell anyone. I couldn't believe it. That afternoon, nursing got Sam out of bed and into a cardiac chair, a big pink ugly gurney-to-chair device they used for patients who can't get into a regular chair. I put Scooby-Doo on TV for

Sam, and while he watched those meddling kids from his pink chair, I used his bedside table to take my exam from his bed.

Sam was released without a trach on Sunday. I returned to school on Monday and got an A on my exam.

When I first decided to go back to school and started at the community college, the finish line seemed impossibly far away. Like I'd never walk across that stage with my master's stole and receive the diploma that would allow me to pursue a career helping others communicate the way I worked with Sam to improve the quality of both our lives. But I did it! Even though I no longer work as a Speech-Language Pathologist (SLP), I worked hard to earn those degrees and, in the process, learned information and techniques that were invaluable to Sam and our ability to communicate effectively.

After graduation, I took a position as the SLP for Ralph Richardson Center in the San Juan Unified School District, the district where Sam and I were both educated. Ralph Richardson is a unique campus for the education of students with profound special needs, often including medical needs. I got to be a part of improving the communication, and therefore connection, between these special students and their families.

## COMMUNICATION

Communication is the window into someone's soul. It's how you know what they want, what they're feeling—who they are. Communicating with Sam was a real-life game of Wheel of Fortune, with the added difficulty of lip-reading. He could understand everything you said, but his short-term memory loss affected his understanding, insight, problem-solving, and planning. He could talk, but his intelligibility varied. He could be loud and project his voice at times, but mostly, he talked quietly, usually whispering.

Quiet speech is a symptom of Parkinson's, and Sam's basal ganglia—the brain area where Parkinson's Disease occurs—was injured. He had Parkinsonism, symptoms of Parkinson's Disease, but not the progressive disease process. It was like his voice had been recalibrated too quietly, and it was difficult for him to turn his voice on. In addition to a lack of voice, he had muscle weakness and poor coordination of his mouth and tongue, similar to someone who's experienced a stroke. That made lip-reading his speech even more difficult than it already was.

Fortunately, Sam's stellar spelling skills played a big role in the way we communicated. Whenever he spoke, and I didn't understand him, I'd first ask him to say one word at a time. Having a clear pause between each word really helped. If I didn't understand the word, I had him spell it one letter at a time. His patience always baffled me. I can't imagine how frustrating it would be to say something but not be understood and then jump through tedious hoops to get your message across.

He never showed his frustration with me, though. He'd repeat and spell for as long as it took for me to get the message. But at times, I would get frustrated and ask for a break. "I really want to know what you have to say, but I'm struggling to understand right now. Can we take a quick break and try again in a minute?" It was important to me that he knew that I valued what he had to say and the effort it took.

Context was tremendously important for quickly understanding what he was saying. If I asked him a question, we were talking about a known subject, or doing some sort of task or activity, understanding him became far easier. The real difficulty came when he had something completely novel to say. These were usually the most interesting things, and I was always so interested in what he was thinking that I'd do whatever I could to stay patient enough to understand him.

When I really couldn't figure out what he was saying, I'd bust out our special alphabet board. I created a version using the transparent front sleeve of a binder for stability, a piece of paper, and a black Sharpie and wrote the alphabet in a grid in alphabetical order with all the vowels highlighted in yellow on the left side to make navigating easier. Deficits in his visual processing added to the challenge, as did the tremor in his right hand and arm. Sam didn't like using it, so it was more of a last resort. He just wanted to talk. Whether we used the alphabet board or speech, we always had our trusty "one for yes, two for no" to confirm or deny. It was our first form of communication, and it was our failsafe.

Sam tended to have good speech days and less successful speech days. The staff and I tried to take advantage of those good days because it was so interesting to know what he had to say. He was often quite verbal in the morning when the nursing staff was tending to him, and they'd tell me about it when I got there. It was usually just casual conversation, but coming from him, it always felt special. Sam was even able to make some contributions to this memoir, which I started writing in 2019.

To illustrate Sam's cognitive and language ability despite his difficulty with speech, I want to share a Father's Day card he dictated to me for his dad. This took the better part of an hour and required using the alphabet board. I had no idea where he was going with this, so I didn't have any context to help me. I kept reminding him this was a Father's Day card to bring him back to the point.

> *To my father,*
>
> *There is an evil monster that lurks in the tower. All the King's horses and all the King's men couldn't destroy the evil monster but then came the King who said, 'All my horses and all my men played a rough game of polo and, and we defeated the alpha. All of us ought to join my army.*

*All of the land that is spent feeding our forces and otherwise is land worth sacrificing.' Not even if I say the magic words could an army defeat you with the power of your fatherly love. You have equipped me with the same weapon. Happy Father's Day. I love you, Dad.*

*SAM*

CHAPTER THIRTEEN

# SUTTER, OUR
# SECOND HOME

While I and his primary caregivers at Care Meridian had a good grasp on communicating with Sam, or rather, understanding his expressive communication, communicating with novel listeners was another story. Whenever he was in the hospital, this was a problem. During the years we were at Care Meridian, Sutter Roseville Medical Center, seven miles away, was the hospital Sam went to when he got sick. He was first hospitalized there in 2009 for aspiration pneumonia and was a patient there more times than I can count. I'd estimate that until the complications of a 2016 surgery, he was there two to three times a year. After the surgery, it was more like three to four, finally culminating in about eight times in his last year.

We were well known all over the hospital, from the security guards to the cafeteria staff, from nursing, doctors, radiology, and phlebotomists to various therapists, all the way to housekeeping, everyone knew, or at least knew of Sam—and by extension, everyone knew me.

One time, my grandparents came by the hospital to take me to lunch, and we were stopped three or four times on our way to the cafeteria by random hospital staff who wanted an update on Sam. Another time, a nurse from the interventional radiology department bought my breakfast, and an incredible nurse, Kyle, came in on his day off to bring us a copy of his favorite book, a zombie book, that he thought Sam would enjoy. He did.

In 2018, Sam was hospitalized for a mysterious fever and admitted to the second-floor telemetry unit, where he ended up spending his birthday. His amazing nurse, Bobbi—a member of the Air Force Reserves—printed out a happy birthday sign for his wall. All the staff and many hospital staff visitors came in to sign it and wish Sam a happy birthday. It was *beyond touching*.

Depending on what unit Sam was on, the nurses either worked eight- or twelve-hour shifts. Typically, ICU and ER nurses work twelves, and floor nurses work eights. What this meant for me was that whenever he was in the ICU, I always stayed past shift change at 7:00 p.m. to make sure we knew the nurse and, if not, that he or she was oriented to Sam. It was important that they knew how to communicate with him and had knowledge of his level of understanding and cognition.

"Sam understands everything you say," I always told them. "He just won't remember it because he has no short-term memory. Make sure you always tell him who you are and what you're doing because even if you told him earlier, he won't remember. Sometimes, he confabulates and thinks he's being held hostage."He can move his right arm and give you a thumbs up or thumbs down or another finger if you make him angry. We use one finger for yes and two fingers for no. As long as you always set him up by saying one for yes or two for no, you'll get an accurate answer. He can talk, but he can be hard to understand, so we always have the fingers as a backup."

Although my routine completely changed whenever Sam was in the hospital, my own health and fitness were still important to me. I also have a really hard time sitting still for very long. Packed in my "go bag" for those late-night emergency calls was a resistance band. I used it with Sam, helping him keep up his strength and range of motion in his right arm, and I used it to keep myself moving. Sam and I would take turns being the other's anchors for back rows, and I used the chair for Bulgarian split squats and dips.

I even trained for two marathons at the hospital. Sutter Roseville is conveniently located in a nice neighborhood and is right across the street from the entrance to Roseville's multi-purpose trail. On days I planned to run, I'd typically wear my running clothes to the hospital and pack clean clothes. First, I'd spend time with Sam, making sure everything was okay and that his nurse was oriented to him. I'd either go out for my run before the doctors' rounds started or wait until they'd finished so I wouldn't miss anything important. As long as all was well, I'd head to the trail, never being more than three miles away at any given point.

If it was a short run, I'd use the benches along the trail for some resistance training: step-ups, Bulgarian split squats, pushups, and dips. Longer runs were just runs, and I got to know the local trail and neighborhoods well. These runs and time in nature were an amazing relief to the hours upon hours of stale hospital life, plus the fears and anxieties that grew with each hospitalization.

For longer runs, I'd loop back to the hospital and check-in. Even though the nurse could just call me, it made me feel better to pop in every hour or so. The longest run I ever did from the hospital was eighteen miles. My friend Elyse was training for the same marathon as me, and instead of meeting our running group in Folsom, she came to the hospital to run with me.

Life in and out of the hospital wasn't ideal, but it was about to get a lot more trying.

## SURGERY

Sam had recurrent pneumonia, and his lungs were colonized by the nasty kinds of superbugs you hear about on the news. These required powerful IV antibiotics whenever their number reached infection level. I suspected that pneumonia from these superbugs would take him out.

Due to his inability to swallow and his severe reflux, Sam had a special kind of feeding tube called a JG-tube. The standard G-tube, which goes through the abdomen directly to the stomach, had a smaller tube within it that had to be directed by an interventional radiologist into the jejunum, a portion of the small intestine, bypassing the stomach.

His meds were administered to the G-tube, and his more voluminous tube feedings went into the jejunum in order to prevent aspiration pneumonia from reflux. Each tube was accessed through a different port at the outside end of the tube.

The problem, though, was the way in which Sam's tube had been initially placed in Bethesda. They didn't do anything wrong, but because it was initially only meant to serve as a G-tube, the angle of the tract was such that the jejunal tubing kept backing itself out over time and winding up in the stomach. This defeated the J-tube's purpose. Even if you accessed the J-tube through the J-port, the feeding still went to the stomach rather than the safer jejunum and led to more occurrences of aspiration pneumonia through reflux.

The solution? Place a separate J-tube that could be positioned optimally, which would have the added benefit of not having to be changed in interventional radiology every three months. He would have two independent tubes, and his tube feeding would have nowhere to go but to the intestines and south. Seems simple, but no. It ended up being anything but simple.

Sam's surgeon at the Mather VA, Dr. Baker, was double board-certified and a former Recon Marine. He had an impressive graying beard and always looked like he was ready to head off on an adventure with Bear Grylls. We couldn't have asked for better. Just being in Dr. Baker's presence gave me hope and confidence. I felt like he was the right guy and that I'd made the right decision for Sam. Sam was admitted on the Thursday afternoon before a Friday surgery, and I had planned to take personal days from work through Tuesday, the planned day of his release back to Care Meridian.

Both our sets of parents were with me in the large surgical waiting room during the surgery. A close family friend picked up food from Panera for everyone, and I mostly read Stephen King's crime thriller, *Mr. Mercedes,* while we waited. After about five hours, Dr. Baker came out to give a good report.

The surgery was onerous due to an extensive amount of scar tissue, but everything looked good, and Sam was in recovery. It was late afternoon already, so rather than attempt to take him off the ventilator and risk overnight complications, we'd wait until the next morning. I was good with this plan because keeping him on the vent meant keeping him sedated, and I wouldn't have to worry about his orientation and behavior. After orienting the evening ICU nurses, I went home to get a good night's sleep. Like a new mother naps when her new baby naps, when Sam was doing well in the hospital, I took advantage of it to make sure I could get a shower and a good night of sleep.

The next day was the big task of waking him up and getting him off the ventilator. To get Sam off the vent, he had to be alert enough to prove he could breathe on his own. They stopped the sedation, but he was still really drowsy and not alert enough to pull the tube. I knew this was just a normal sleepy day for Sam. He often went into these super deep, scary sleeps after a fever, a bad night, or, hey, apparently when recovering from surgery.

I told the surgical resident I had an idea to get him to wake up. Sam had a paradoxical reaction to benzodiazepines—meds like Xanax, Valium, and Ativan. Instead of these meds having a sedating effect on him, they acted as stimulants for him. He actually took Ativan daily like you and I have our morning coffee.

I told the resident and proposed giving him Ativan through the IV. My estimate is they could extubate within twenty minutes. Worst case scenario, he'd just keep sleeping. His airway was protected by the ventilator. When the resident ran it by the attending, it was a go. I got to give the residents a lesson in neuropharmacology, and Sam was off the vent and extubated in fifteen minutes.

The next evening, I planned to leave the VA to visit a close, elderly friend in another hospital across town. My pastor's mom, Roberta, and I had been dear friends for about five years. She'd been in the hospital for a few weeks, and before Sam's surgery, I'd been visiting her, her condition waxing and waning.

My pastor planned to spend some time with his family while I stayed with Roberta, but I had to tell him I needed to be with Sam. Roberta was not doing well, but I had a sick feeling about Sam, and my place was with him. Roberta had been a caregiver herself and loved Sam dearly; she'd understand.

After giving his gut a full day to rest, they began a trickle tube feeding. Several hours in, he developed a low-grade fever and looked a bit yellow to me. By the next day, he was definitely jaundiced with a high fever of 103.5°F. His belly was rigid and distended. For the first time since the early days in Bethesda, I had that "How is this my reality?" feeling in my gut.

I came in the next morning around 7:15 a.m. with the only breakfast I could stomach: coffee and chocolate milk (our comfort drink) from Cooper's Coffee in Folsom. Sam wasn't any better. Then, suddenly, he was doing much worse. In minutes, he went from having a slightly elevated heart rate and oxygen saturation slipping to tachycardia, oxygen below ninety and dropping, and BP dropping. The ICU staff, doctors, nurses, and respiratory therapists were all over him. They told me they were going to have to re-intubate and kicked me out to the waiting room.

Panic rose in me as I waited all alone in the huge surgical waiting room. I paced. I prayed. I sat. I paced some more. Through tears, I texted my pastor. We'd been keeping each other updated on our respective patient's conditions. I needed him to pray for Sam, and I wanted an update on Roberta. He replied back promptly. Roberta died overnight. He had been with her. He was praying for Sam.

I was crushed, but they were still in the midst of saving Sam. I didn't know who to cry for, who to pray for, what to do. I was too numb, and the situation was moving too fast for me to call anyone just yet. I needed to wait until I knew something. Either he was okay, or he wasn't. I pulled out the Bible app on my phone and just started reading. I was trying to pray but couldn't keep my mind from racing. Reading scripture at least gave me something to hold onto—something to do.

Maybe fifteen minutes later—also known as an eternity—one of the residents came to get me. Sam was okay. They intubated him and put him back on the vent. The unprocessed stomach content was compressing his lungs, which caused respiratory distress. He was stable but critical. We had a long way to go.

Now we had his respiratory system to contend with on top of his digestive system, and because he'd just recently had a breathing tube, the window for getting him off the vent to remove the breathing tube would be shorter than the typical ten- to fourteen-day window. If we waited longer, Sam risked having permanent vocal fold damage. We were now seriously looking at the possibility of a trach.

But his gut wasn't responding to the feeding. The immediate, conservative treatment was to hook his G-tube up to suction and drain his stomach content to relieve pressure and the burden from his gut. They inserted a nasogastric tube—a tube up the nose and fed into the stomach for the same purpose. He was no longer getting any feeding, and we had two sources draining his stomach content. Aspiration pneumonia, the whole reason we did the surgery in the first place, was now a concern.

It was a long, uneventful day, at least compared to the morning managing his belly, lungs, and temperature. He had acquired aspiration pneumonia, which was now being treated by IV antibiotics, and his gut developed an ileus, a temporarily paralyzed portion of the intestines.

Sam became more jaundiced over the course of the day, and due to being back on the ventilator, he was sedated again. They continued draining his stomach to relieve the abdominal pressure affecting his liver and lungs. The resident on overnight sent me home to rest around 10:00 p.m., with a promise to keep a close eye on him.

Around 1:00 a.m., the phone woke me out of a dead sleep. Our resident. Sam wasn't responding well enough to the conservative treatment, and the attending surgeon suspected a bowel obstruction. They were taking him to surgery because waiting until morning would only mean more damage if there was indeed an intestinal obstruction.

There's nothing quite like the adrenal rush of being awakened in the middle of the night by a ringing phone to be told your medically fragile husband is headed in for emergency surgery. I jumped in the car and made it to the hospital in no time. But I stupidly didn't contact anyone. I didn't have to be alone, but for some reason, I felt I could or should handle it on my own because it was the middle of the night, and I didn't want to bother anyone. If I were my family, I'd be pretty pissed with me. My in-laws never said anything, trusting me to be the driver of Sam's care, but I got an earful from my mom for not calling.

I was trying hard not to panic, but as I stood there holding Sam's hand, I knew this could be the end. I held him as best as I could with all his medical accessories in the way of the hug I really needed. The anesthesiologist came in to prep Sam and talked to me. He had a fantastic way of talking to distract and comfort me. It turned out we were neighbors and had a funny story about our mailman and a wild turkey.

They took Sam into surgery, and I sat in his room watching TV, still, to my shame, not contacting the family. I feel like I must have repressed the waiting as I don't remember much of anything other than being scared and praying over and over again that Sam would be okay. The surgeon, an African man whose name I sadly don't remember, came to give me the update. Sam was okay.

There was no obstruction. He'd developed abdominal compartment syndrome, increased pressure in the abdomen from the first surgery. Sam's belly was so distended that the doctor couldn't even close the abdomen. Sam had a gaping incision still open; the only thing between the outside world and his intestines was a layer of medical-grade plastic protecting it. If the surgeon had tried to close him with sutures, the pressure from his belly would have ripped the sutures right out.

The surgical team brought him back to the room and got him all situated. He was stable, and once again, the resident sent me home to sleep. The entire ordeal took less than three hours, and I was back home in bed long before the first light. Several months later, we ran into this surgeon while at a follow-up appointment with Dr. Baker. He was amazed at how good Sam looked and confessed to me that he didn't think Sam was going to make it off the table that night. I'd been scared, but I didn't know how close I'd come to losing him.

What followed was a long road to discharge, but the worst of this hospitalization was over. Sam received a bio-mesh, basically a graft from pig flesh over his open abdomen. The wound would slowly heal itself from the inside out.

To my consternation, he did end up with a trach, which required yet another surgery. Even though I understood the necessity for it from a medical standpoint, the trach was terribly upsetting to me. It felt like a huge setback, a defeat even. Sam would come off the ventilator more quickly and easily with a trach than without, and it could always be removed. Getting him off the ventilator, breathing on his own, and protecting the health of his vocal folds were the top priorities.

As well as I understood from a medical perspective, I was also concerned about his quality of life long term. Speech was already arduous for Sam, and I worried about his ability to speak post-trach. You'll never realize how important simple communication is between you and someone you love until it's taken away. We'd still have one for yes, and two for no, but at least for a time, I wouldn't get to hear his voice or know what he was thinking. A crushing blow at a time when I already felt beat to a pulp.

As beat up and defeated as I felt, Sam was a champ. He was in great condition when they wheeled him into the OR for this one. The ever-helpful Sam even squeezed his own AMBU bag, ventilating himself, as they transported him from his ICU room ventilator to the ventilator in the OR.

After a month in ICU, Sam was discharged back to Care Meridian with a trach, IV nutrition called TPN, and a wound-vac dressing on his abdomen. It felt incredible to be out of the hospital and back home. I had developed quite a fondness for the nursing staff and the residents at the VA, but I sorely missed our Care Meridian staff and the peace of life outside the ICU.

It's really hard to accurately document this time and the many, many ups and downs. I received so much support from family, friends, and coworkers at Ralph Richardson. I had to take family medical leave, as there was no way I could return to work. My co-workers brought me bags of snacks, on-the-go meals, and comfort items to get me through. Friends from church came by the hospital to drop off care packages and hot meals. Add to that medical soup the fact that I was recovering from a knee injury, and my physical therapist was just a few miles down the street. Our moms and a couple of friends sat with Sam so I could leave for my appointment and not worry about leaving him alone during the day.

My friend lived just a few minutes from the hospital and visited often. One day, Suzanne sat across from me with her back to the window that looked out at the VA campus as I perched on the edge of Sam's bed. I was beyond overwhelmed and totally broke down, telling her I wasn't ready to lose Sam. There was so much to recover from—so far to go until he was stable. Sam, right hand in soft restraints to prevent him from pulling at his breathing tube, rubbed my thigh as I tearfully expressed my fears. She reminded me of how God had brought him through before—how many times he'd proven the doctors wrong.

# CHAPTER FOURTEEN

# FURTHER COMPLICATIONS

The post-ICU honeymoon lasted one day. On the second day home from the hospital, Sam's nurse noticed a leak in his belly. Stool was leaking through a small hole, about the diameter of a stir stick. Within a few hours, a second hole opened up, and it was back to Sutter Roseville. Based on his significant history and the complexity of his current situation, Dr. Aghili, who saw Sam in the ER, admitted him to the ICU. He had a trach but was off the vent. If there was room in the ICU, Dr. Aghili always preferred to have Sam there in order to keep a closer eye on him.

The leaks were called fistulas and were responsible for yet another near-death experience. Managing the leaking stool was an ongoing and not very successful project. Stool and skin are not a healthy combination, and on day two in the ICU, the wound care nurse and I were trying to rig up something to manage the leak yet protect the integrity of the skin around the area.

While the wound care nurse was working, Sam's monitor kept alarming due to his dropping blood pressure. His ICU nurse promptly ran IV fluids to increase his BP, but within minutes, the IV fluids were coming straight out of the fistulas. He added pressers (medication to raise BP) and kept the fluids running. His blood pressure was tanking due to significant fluid loss. He needed fluids and pressers to support his blood pressure, but the fluid was practically running straight through his fistulas. It was like trying to keep a leaky cup full. The nurse was amazing and stayed so cool that despite my years of experience with Sam's medical emergencies, it took me a while to realize this was a very serious situation. I called in our families.

After a few hours and several bags of fluids and rounds of pressers, I suggested slowing down the rate of the fluids to maybe increase absorption before it leaked out. The nurse liked my idea and gave it a try. It worked. By the end of the day, Sam had stabilized, but since the fistulas were an ongoing problem, hypotension from fluid loss would continue to be a concern. Thank God Dr. Aghili had chosen to admit Sam to the ICU, where he could be carefully monitored. This was a close call, and it would be a while before he was truly out of the woods.

The plan was for the surgical team to keep monitoring the fistulas. But as long as Sam was stable, we were waiting for a bed to open up at the VA so he would be back under Dr. Baker's care. Sam was transferred back to the Mather VA about ten days after being admitted to the Sutter ICU, and fortunately, he didn't require another surgery. He would, however, very likely need his entire GI tract re-plumbed after a few months of rest.

With this knowledge, I resigned my position with the school district. I didn't want the thought of going back to work and this likely surgery over my head all summer. I didn't need to work, but I did need to be with Sam. I knew that whenever I lost Sam, I wasn't going to wish that

I'd worked more or that I was further along in my career. All I would want was more time with Sam. And I had the choice to control my time with him—for now.

The fistula care came mostly down to wound care. The wound care nurse saw him every day, sometimes twice a day. Besides her, I was the number one expert on how to manage it. Before he was discharged back to Care Meridian, one of their nurses and the Director of Nursing came to get a hands-on lesson from the wound care nurse. Sam would also have monthly follow-up visits with both her and Dr. Baker. Eventually, with a lot of TLC and trial and error, the entire abdominal wound closed, Sam was able to get off of IV nutrition and tolerate tube feedings again, and best of all, he didn't need the major follow-up surgery.

It was just another long, scary chapter, but God saw us through. Sam was meant to be with us for a while longer. He still had lots of love to give.

Post-injury, Sam wasn't a morning person despite the double-windowed room letting in the morning light. The staff let him stay in bed until 10:00 or 11:00 a.m., but he still had early morning nursing needs. Morning meds were given through his feeding tube, and he had to be catheterized (good luck sleeping through that). Sam could move his head, right arm, and leg on his own but wasn't able to change positions in bed, leaving him vulnerable to pressure sores, so he had to be turned.

The fact that in eleven years at Care Meridian, he never got a pressure sore is a great testament to the high quality of care he received there. Whenever Sam was in the hospital, the doctors and nurses commented on what great care he must receive based on the health of his skin and his teeth. The acknowledgment gave me joy because I took great pride in the quality of his care and his great hygiene and grooming.

He got showered three days a week, so those days started a bit earlier than he'd have preferred. But if he was confabulating, caring for Sam in the morning could be difficult. When he thought the staff was there to harm him, he'd try to bat their hands away and do anything but cooperate. Fortunately, it wasn't an everyday occurrence, and he could only use one arm. He was usually quite helpful, even chatty, in the mornings. I loved coming in around 11:00 a.m. to hear about Sam having a talkative morning and the charming things he had to say.

The CNAs would get him up into his wheelchair between 10:00 and 11:00 a.m.. If I got there while he was still in bed, I'd squeeze myself in with him for a morning snuggle. Once he was up, we looked for something entertaining or productive to do. Mostly, we read a lot and attended Sam's therapies. Many days, he had speech, occupational, and physical therapy. Usually, it was a combination of the two together, as it took two people to get him onto either the mat table, the patio swing, or the tilt table. Sometimes I was that second person.

Twice a week in the afternoon during his last couple of years, Sam was part of an exercise group run by the therapists. He followed along and did the prescribed exercises as best as he could with his right arm, and whoever was helping him (usually me) would take his left arm through the movements. He enjoyed the exercise, and his strength and coordination with his right arm really improved.

One of the long-term patients, Kelly, was deaf. At the end of each exercise session, everyone would finger-sign the alphabet. Sam couldn't remember the letters, but he was pretty good at making the shapes. We also learned some other signs, usually based on a theme. It was a fun and creative way of improving everyone's ability to communicate with Kelly, and it doubled as fantastic fine- and gross-motor movement practice for the patients.

Fridays were special because it was music therapy day. At 11:00, the great room was transformed into the Care Meridian band jam session.

Celeste, the music therapist, brought in all sorts of instruments for people to play. Music therapy was normally a family affair for us because I often had at least one niece or nephew with me, my parents came often, and my grandparents came almost every week. My grandparents kept coming weekly, even when I was up north in Redding for an internship. When Roberta was still living, she and I met for coffee in the morning then she met me at Sam's for music.

Sam loved music and had been a drummer as a teenager. Over the years, Celeste and I figured out the best drum setups for Sam. She had a cymbal stand that could sit on a bedside table, which Sam loved to use, but then one day, he asked for his snare. We figured out that when positioned just right, we could get an ocean drum (a handheld drum filled with ball bearings) to sound like a snare. Now Sam had a two-piece drum kit. His tremors made holding onto a normal stick nearly impossible, and they constantly slipped out of his hand. After lots of trial and error, I rigged up the perfect drumstick using road bike handlebar grip tape to build up the handle. One of the characteristics of a right-hemisphere brain injury is a denial of injury. Sam would often ask for his second stick. Even though he couldn't move his left hand or arm, I always made sure his left hand was holding a stick.

Sam definitely still had the drummer's touch. He knew what he wanted to do musically and, quite often, even pulled it off. The therapists and my grandma and I would look at each other with raised eyebrows, like, "Damn, Sam."

When we weren't in therapy, Sam and I might watch TV, but mostly we tried to entertain ourselves. I loved doing anything physical with Sam— always trying to keep him progressing, or at least not regressing—both physically and cognitively. A big favorite activity of ours, which often included other patients or my niece and nephew, was balloon volleyball in the great room. Every now and then, I'd pull out our wooden and magnetic chess set. The magnets kept Sam's shaky arm from knocking all the pieces off the board, and I'd put a medical glove on his right hand to improve his grip. He could play chess, but it usually took a lot of patience on my part waiting for him to make his move.

Whether we were in Sam's room or, ideally, outside, enjoying the scenic property, we read a lot. He was capable of reading, but his injury made the visual processing of trying to read a novel impossible, so I always read aloud. I lost count of how many times I read *Harry Potter*. We read the *Eragon* books, *Lord of the Rings*, *Ender's Game*, and the *Red Rising* trilogy, among others. Sometimes, I'd start reading a book on my own and realize Sam would be into it, so I'd set it aside to read together.

Around midday, Sam had his meds and other more private nursing tasks. I'd usually give him some privacy while I ate my lunch.

Besides therapy, reading, and physical activities, I loved grooming Sam. It sounds kind of weird, but I loved leaning his wheelchair back and giving him a good shave, and I especially loved cutting his hair. Marines have to have their hair cut every week, and before his injury, we went to the barbershop. I learned a lot from watching in person, but I learned even more from trial and error (it was never terrible). And I found a love of barber videos on YouTube. Grooming Sam gave me a sense of control when so much was out of my control. Sam was a pretty boy, and he knew it, so he enjoyed the pampering and the compliments it garnered him.

His active part of the day ended around 4:00 p.m. He experienced neural fatigue, which is a kind of whole-body lethargy beyond what you and I experience in our afternoon energy slump. Sam typically went back to bed around this time and was down for the day. He normally didn't sleep, but his body and mind needed rest. Depending on the day, I'd usually climb in bed with him, the CNAs leaving space for me.

These afternoon cuddles in bed were some of my favorite times. As affectionate as Sam always was, a wheelchair really isn't very cuddly. In bed, our warm bodies could make contact in a way they never could out of bed anymore. We'd usually lie with his right arm around me, my head perched on his chest. He'd always bend his head down to kiss the top of my head. I was in my favorite place. It reminded me of laying together on his futon as teenagers or a tender, long, tight hug in the kitchen in our apartment. It was nothing sexual–just the oxytocin-producing warmth of our closeness flooding my system.

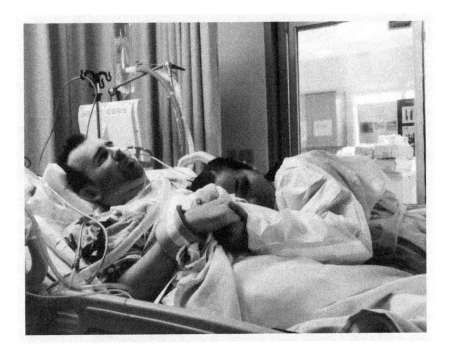

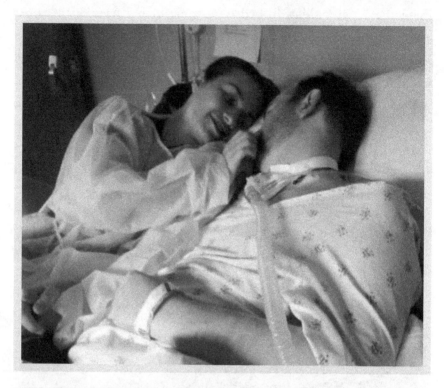

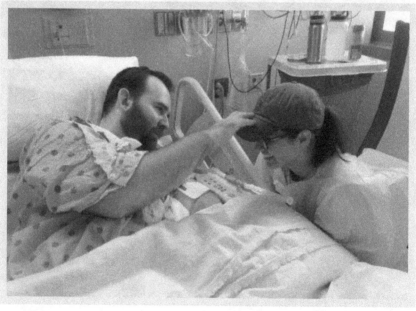

## IT WASN'T ALL CUDDLES AND HARRY POTTER

Sam's TBI was at its most heartbreaking when he had a sad or scary confabulation. One December day, my mom and I were meeting at Sam's in the evening to carpool to a high school Christmas performance.

"Hey, hon," I said as I started to climb in bed with him, but then—.

"STOP!" Sam commanded. "Erin is dead! My girlfriend is dead in bed with me. You need to call 911!"

"Sam, honey, look at me. *I'm* Erin. Feel the bed next to you. There's no one in bed with you. I'm Erin. I'm here to cuddle with you for a few minutes.""No! You're an imposter! Erin's dead!"

No amount of trying to convince him that no one was in bed with him or that I was the real Erin would do. Instead, he got more angry, more fearful, more tortured. So I tried leaving his room for a while and coming back, hoping his short-term memory loss would work in my favor...

Nope. This was a bad one.

He was in terrible distress, and I was not helping. My mom arrived and tried to change his focus, but he was fixated on his dead girlfriend. Eventually, I just had to leave and tell the staff what was going on. He was safe and, thankfully, wouldn't remember this in the morning.


## MENTAL HEALTH

Sam's mental health was always a big concern for me, but my own was another story. I did a good job distracting myself with Sam, school, training, and, let's not discount good ol' denial.

My maternal grandma, Nana Connie, died of breast cancer just before I turned four. I only have a couple of memories of her. Mostly, what I got from her (or rather, the memory of her from my mom and my aunt) is a fear of being mentally ill. Nana Connie had both bipolar disorder and paranoid schizophrenia. My mom and her siblings suffered a traumatic and unstable childhood as a result, and they have their own mental health battles, including PTSD from this childhood. From a young age, I've been terrified to become like Nana Connie. If you don't have your mind, what are you left with?

Because of this, I waited way too long to get the help I needed.

Deployment mode was a good coping strategy at the time. The ability to compartmentalize is what allows us not to be buried by every problem, big or small. Deployment mode, however, became avoidance and the way I dealt with trauma. After my initial trauma with Sam's injury, I had the repeated trauma of hospitalization after hospitalization, late-night phone call after late-night phone call, and being THE guardian of Sam's life and, ultimately, his survival.

This created a depression-prone, anxiety-riddled existence for me. When I went back to college in my late twenties, my professors and friends pointed out that I had symptoms of ADHD. Then, in grad school, we had a double methods class with Mrs. Oldenburg, where the cohort sat around in a circle discussing our clinic clients for two hours. About halfway through, we'd take a fifteen- to twenty-minute break, which Mrs. O announced based on my inability to sit still. She'd look over at me kindly. "Erin, are you ready for a wiggle break?"

I'd experienced both depression and anxiety in the past, but they were always situational. It's clear to me now that since Sam was first injured, I'd been on a mental health roller coaster, barely keeping my head above water. Between his dire circumstances, his many and changing needs, and my profound sense of loss of control, my own stable emotional center wafted between competing demands. I could barely focus. I needed to be busy all the time. I constantly waited for the next shoe to drop, for something terrible to happen to Sam.

In 2012, about five years after Sam's injury, I was on my way to my apartment from Care Meridian when I started having trouble breathing. Thinking it was asthma, I took a couple of hits off my inhaler. But by the time I got home, the symptoms had worsened. I couldn't catch my breath. My hands were tingling and becoming hard to move. I kept thinking about the patient at Care Meridian who had an anoxic brain injury from an asthma attack. I took another hit from the inhaler and tried to calm my breathing.

It didn't work. The tingling was worse. I was losing control of my hands and had to fight to open them and move my fingers. Not being able to fully exhale meant carbon dioxide was building up in my bloodstream and causing carpopedal spasms.

Panic rising, I called my mom to take me to the hospital. The periphery of my vision went dark. We were just a few minutes away from Sutter Roseville Hospital when I told her I was starting to black out. I managed to stay conscious, but the tingling and loss of control of my hands had spread to my forearms. The uncontrollable flexing of my forearms was so strong it felt like I was going to tear ligaments in my wrists.

I have no memory of Mom helping me walk into the emergency room or waiting to be seen. When they took my vitals, I was sure my oxygen saturation would be low, but it was a strong and healthy 99%. My heart rate, however, was 225 beats per minute, more than triple my resting heart rate.

The treatment for the asthma attack I *thought* I was having was a stimulant, which made the anxiety attack I was *actually* having far worse. Just seeing that my oxygen saturation was good was a great comfort, and being in the safety of the hospital helped to calm me down. I was given a paper bag to breathe into and was fine by the time I saw the doctor. Given my life circumstances, he highly recommended I get into therapy.

My primary care doctor had made the same therapy recommendation time and time again, but my deployment-mode-tough-girl wall was too strong. I didn't see the need for therapy. Subconscious denial and fear of being like my grandma kept me from getting help for far too long, and the issues only festered.

By early 2016, hyperventilation and the resulting carpopedal spasms had become a common issue. I knew it was related to anxiety, but in my denial, I couldn't identify one specific source of it. Sam, hospitals, medical urgency, and midnight emergency phone calls were just my life. Besides, I rationalized the anxiety attacks tended to come on either when I was driving or otherwise just hanging out.

In addition to the hyperventilation in 2016 amidst Sam's GI surgery crisis, I began having heart palpitations. The first time it happened, we were having a chill reading session in the ICU when my heart suddenly started racing and skipping beats. This kept happening, always while I was relaxing, usually at home in the evening or as I lay in bed to go to sleep. I had a battery of cardiac tests done, and although I have a very slight murmur, my heart was in great shape, and these palpitation episodes were anxiety-induced. I should seek therapy, they recommended. Mmmmm…not yet.

In early 2017, my mood had really taken a turn. I had stopped working, and my life had been solely focused on Sam's health since the previous spring. Other than my own physical training and family, I didn't have anything to focus on outside of Sam. My motivation and drive to do anything I didn't have to do completely tanked. People who saw me daily, like Sam's therapists, expressed concerns about me. I didn't seem my normal chipper self. It was like the volume dial on my personality had been set too low. When I wasn't with Sam, all I did was lie on the couch and watch TV or read, not wanting to keep up with my normal evening gym routines or socialize.

Finally, my sister, Ali, convinced me to talk to my doctor about anxiety and depression. We shared a doctor, and she had recently been put on a med for anxiety and depression, which had a tremendous impact on how she felt and was able to live. I was forced to face my lifelong fear of mental health straight on, but my sister's enthusiasm and concern convinced me.

As I was in the office with Dr. R. talking about my symptoms, I completely broke down, just like I had with Dr. Duncan at Kentfield years before. I was hyperventilating and crying uncontrollably. Based on that meltdown, she added Xanax to the prescription of Celexa for anxiety and depression.

I got to test out the Xanax just a few days later when my grandpa called on Mother's Day morning just as I was on my way to church. Seeing my grandparent's cell phone number alarmed me. Even more alarming was that Grandpa, not Grandma (their usual spokesperson), was on the line. They never use their cell phone! I thought, feeling my heart rate start to climb. He was trying to track down my dad, he said. Grandma was okay, but she'd had a stroke, and they were at Mercy San Juan Hospital. I started making weepy, voice-strangled calls to my sister and then to my maternal great-grandma, whom I hated giving the stroke news and sadly telling her we wouldn't be making our Mother's Day visit. By then, my hands were tingling, and I had no finger dexterity. I took my first Xanax. When I arrived at the hospital, I was able to be present for my grandpa and family, not having my own crisis.

The meds made a tremendous difference, but by early 2020, I was starting to have difficulty with anxiety and depression again. My doctor referred me to a psychiatrist to manage my psych meds and insisted that I finally get into therapy. The timing couldn't have been more perfect.

# CHAPTER FIFTEEN

# NEARING THE END

In his final year, Sam was hospitalized for a part of every month save one, but returned to Care Meridian each time. Before this 2019-2020 stint, his three to five hospitalizations a year were usually for a combination of pneumonia and UTIs. In that last year, though, something changed. A mystery source of bacteria was making him very sick.

I ran the Marine Corps Marathon in October 2019 in the middle of that run of hospitalizations. Let me tell you, I'd rather run 26.2 miles every month than have Sam in and out of the hospital like that.

The basic procedure for him going to the hospital was to work him up in the ER with chest x-rays and your typical labs (urinalysis, sputum culture, blood cultures, and white blood count). The higher the WBC, the sicker he was. A higher-than-normal WBC indicates infection. As familiar and comfortable as I was with these procedures, I spent much of our 2019-2020 time in the ER with my heart in my stomach, waiting to find out how bad it was this time.

These tests meant hours and hours in the ER. It was clear he'd be admitted, but it takes time for a room to become available, so typically, his nurse would order Sam a bed with an air mattress to help prevent pressure sores and get him off the ER gurney ASAP. My special accommodations included nothing but a hard plastic chair.

The urinalysis and cultures would hopefully reveal where bacteria were present: urine, lungs, or blood. Cultures also tell you the type of bacteria growing so you can treat it with an effective antibiotic against it. Doctors start with broad-spectrum IV antibiotics, then get more targeted in a few days when the cultures come back.

The problem and the start of the mystery came from Sam's blood culture. Why did he have bacteria in his blood? Where was it coming from? Not only do doctors need to treat the acute infection, but to prevent a recurrence, they need to find its source. Sam's blood was positive for bacteria, but they couldn't find that type of bacteria anywhere else in his body. The typical culprit would be an infected long-term IV, but the lab tests showed that wasn't the case. With this new Sam mystery, the doctors wracked their brains and mine for the source of this bacteria.

The process of treating Sam usually went like this: Admit to either the ICU or a telemetry unit. Start on broad-spectrum antibiotics and administer his normal meds (there were a lot). Have respiratory see him for trach care, nebulizer treatments, and chest percussion. Nursing followed my lead in getting him out of bed and into a chair once a day, depending on how he felt. The hospitalist, infectious disease doctor, and sometimes the pulmonologist included him in their daily rounds. Once cultures were back, infectious disease would change the IV antibiotics. There were, of course, tons of lab tests every day. Now, due to the mystery bacteria, several other tests like a nuclear study and CTs were also done.

184

When his WBC was normal and his blood cultures negative, they began talking about discharge. Discharge included increasing lengths of IV antibiotic courses. Dr. Lopez, the infectious disease doctor, eventually started Sam on a small, ongoing dose of amoxicillin to help suppress the bacteria, whose source was still a mystery.

About a third of the way through the mystery infection hospitalization, standing in the hallway outside Sam's room, Dr. Lopez dropped a bomb. "Erin, this may be the beginning of the end."

They couldn't identify the source of the bacteria in his blood, and Sam's body could only take so many antibiotics. Antibiotics don't just kill the bad bugs; they kill all the bugs, including the good ones we need for a strong immune system. Eventually, the bacteria would become resistant and the biggest threat to his immune system. At that point, Sam had very little immune system left, and giving him probiotics was like plugging only one of several leaks. The next infection or a bad virus could take him out. See where this is going?

The doctors kept looking for a source of this bacteria in Sam's blood; time and time again, they asked for my input. The only thing I could think of was shrapnel. He had some in his right arm, leg, and plenty in his right hip and abdomen.

When he was first hurt, the shrapnel came out right and left. I could go to lunch and come back to find a new piece working its way out. Finally, a hard, dark lump appeared on his right side about midway between his hip and bottom rib. I was thrilled to have something to point out to the doctors, but when they checked it out, there was no sign of infection or even inflammation.

Eventually, that little guy started to break for the surface when Sam was home at Care Meridian. When it started draining, the nurses put a dressing and bacitracin on it. But the very next day, he spiked a fever and was back in the hospital.

Sam was admitted to the ICU, and his nurse, Aaron, noted the dressing and the wound underneath upon admitting him. When he removed the dressing, there was a foul smell, so he ordered a wound consult. When the wound care nurse came by, our little shrapnel baby was crowning. She gripped it with some forceps, and out it came. A thirteen-year-old piece of shrapnel!

The nurses were stoked. They don't get much war shrapnel in Roseville, California. For the rest of the hospitalization, I was stopped in the halls and the cafeteria by staff members asking about it and wanting to see pictures. If Sgt. Sam wasn't already famous at Sutter Roseville, he was now.

Besides the cool factor, it was also exciting that perhaps we'd finally located the source of bacteria. They cultured the shrapnel, but Sam was on so many antibiotics already he was practically sterile (not really, but nothing could grow). The culture didn't grow anything, but there was still hope that the culprit had been removed. Unfortunately, that wasn't the case. We got a good story out of it, and the legend of Sgt. Sam grew, but the bacteria was back in business about six weeks later. After two or three of these mystery infection hospitalizations, the prognosis worsening with each one, Sam was assigned to the palliative care team.

I'm really good at compartmentalizing my feelings, and as my therapist says, I intellectualize so I don't have to deal with my emotions. If Sam was in a medical crisis, instead of feeling fear and anxiety, I calmly evaluated the situation from a medical standpoint. Later, I might have an anxiety attack or heart palpitations that seemed to come from nowhere. Even when my emotions would get the best of me, my eyes would be dry, and my thoughts clear within a second of talking shop with a doctor or member of Sam's care team.

Palliative care, though, was a different story. Sam's death was inevitable whether he had days, weeks, months, or—as I hoped and prayed for—years. He'd made it this far and overcome so much. Why not this time?

I interacted with two members of the palliative care team. First was Trish, the nurse. She also worked as an instructor at one of the local nursing schools, so I also saw her in that capacity when her students performed various procedures on Sam. We formed a good relationship over time. She wanted to make sure I was taken care of and that I understood not only the severity of Sam's condition but all my options and resources. And she did it in a way that made me feel heard and understood.

Dr. Wong and I, however, did not get along. He made me feel like Sam was a dog that needed to be put down. I understood the gravity of the situation. I wasn't stupid, naive, or blinded by false hope. But Sam was still alive, and no amount of talking to me about his imminent death was going to change anything about the way I treated him or made medical decisions for him.

*They* only saw him when he was sick. *I* knew how much life he had and the quality of life he had outside the hospital. They didn't see him singing and playing the drums during music therapy, playing cards or chess, or even creating flower bouquets. Heck, Sam even had a great quality of life in the hospital. He loved nothing more than cuddling in bed with me and reading, which we had plenty of time to do in the hospital.

During one of these hospitalizations, Dr. Wong asked to meet with me. I asked that Father Danny, one of the chaplains, be present. I didn't want to be alone with Dr. Wong and felt safe with Father Danny. I can't even tell you exactly what we talked about, but all I know is that I ended up needing a Xanax to contend with hyperventilation. After the meeting, I spent a good hour with Father Danny in the small but cheery chapel, just talking and crying harder than I ever had in that hospital.

I couldn't really talk to Sam about this stuff. He didn't understand the gravity of his situation, and even if I could get him to understand it, he'd forget it almost immediately. He understood everything you said; he just had no short-term memory and couldn't project his thoughts toward the future. He would, however, see my puffy, red-rimmed eyes, rub my back, and kiss my hand. There was no better comfort than squeezing my way into Sam's hospital bed, carefully navigating my way around IVs and his catheter tubing, and letting him hold me. Sometimes, I'd even grab his limp left arm and hold that around me as well.

After a stint in the hospital in January 2020, I thought I'd be safe to take a trip down South with my family in mid-February. Mom and I took my car to meet my sister's family at Universal Studios. We were basically just there for Harry Potter, and it didn't disappoint. Then, we drove down to Anaheim to stay at a hotel near Disneyland and spend the next couple of days between Disneyland and California Adventure before driving home.

Brrriiiing, brrriiiiing! Dammit! Best laid plans, right? Around 5:00 a.m. the first morning in Anaheim, I got a call. Sam had a fever, and they were sending him to the hospital. I was 430 miles south. I told his nurse to pass on the info that I was in Southern California and would be there ASAP. This is when the ER staff knowing you really well comes in handy. I knew there would be staff who knew his background and at least vaguely knew how to communicate with him.

Luckily, I got a flight out of John Wayne Airport mid-morning (hot tip: if you can fly into Burbank, Long Beach, or John Wayne instead of LAX, do it). I called Sam's mom so she'd be with him at least until I got there. She didn't know the medical stuff like I did, but we could call or text easily, and I hated the idea of him being alone.

I took an Uber to the airport so my mom didn't have to take me and could drive my car back up in a few days. But just as I was scrambling to get ready, my sister called. She and one of the kids were quite sick. She suspected strep, and they were going to Urgent Care. This trip was really going well.

I landed in Sacramento by late morning, and my grandparents picked me up at the airport. They graciously lent me one of their cars until my mom got back with mine. A little after noon, I joined my mother-in-law in the ER. It may be odd to feel relaxed in a hospital, but aside from knowing the hospital and the staff really well, it was an incredible relief to be with Sam. I'd felt so helpless until I could be there by his side, talking to him, suctioning him, fixing his hair, and generally picking at him like the helper monkey I was.

It was Sam's last hospitalization.

# CHAPTER SIXTEEN

# SHUTDOWN

We started 2020 with that late January to mid-February hospitalization. Sam was home at Care Meridian for about three weeks before the COVID shutdown started. Once the shutdown order was issued on March 15, 2020, I couldn't see him in person and was terrified at the prospect of him going back to the hospital. His amazing therapists, who are like family, made sure we stayed connected, using Facetime on their phones during therapy so that we could see each other.

The therapy room had windows that overlooked the back patio, and Sam's therapists—with approval from the Director of Nursing—set up a kind of drive-thru window during his session. I hung out on the patio looking in through the open screened windows while Sam stood on the tilt table for therapy.

Because he was a good ten feet from the window, he really had to project his voice for me to be able to hear him, which was perfect for speech therapy. He tended to have some of his best speech while upright on the tilt table at about sixty degrees. My last picture with Sam was from this day: me outside the window and Sam and his therapists through the screened window inside.

On April 2nd, 2020, I was out for a bike ride when I got a text from our SLP, Sue, asking if I could Facetime during therapy. I pulled off the main road into a neighborhood, laid my bike down on the sidewalk, and sat on the curb across the street from a family doing yard work. I had a great conversation with Sam. He was happy, alert, and speaking loudly and clearly enough for me to understand him. Our last conversation.

The next day, he spiked a fever in the late afternoon. He'd had a perfectly healthy day. His therapists, who'd had a great session with him just a few hours before, were shocked. His nurses began his fever protocol: Tylenol, ice packs, and, at minimum, hourly temperature checks. Despite their efforts, his temperature was only going up. After two hours of not responding to treatment, they called the doctor, followed by 911.

The final phone call came around 7:30 p.m. Of the multitude of traumatic phone calls I've received, this is the one I don't remember. I have zero recollection of what I was doing, which nurse called me, or even the oh-so-familiar drive up Sierra College Blvd. to the hospital, mind typically racing with prayer.

My memory starts as I walked into the eerily deserted ER waiting room, heart in my throat, with no idea if they'd even let me in. Normally packed with the local injured and sick, there was only a nurse and a security guard positioned there to direct traffic.

Being so well known by Sutter Roseville staff, they let me right in. This was my first indication that the situation was dire. Sam was in a special isolation room with a sliding glass door, which he'd been a resident of countless times due to the scary bacteria living in him. I was allowed to sit just outside and look through the glass, poking my head in to speak to him as staff entered and exited. Knowing all the nurses, doctors, x-ray techs, and respiratory therapists attending to him was an incredible comfort.

Sam's temperature was a brain-boiling 106°, and his chest x-rays came back with ground glass opacities (doctor-speak for gray hazy spots), hallmark signs of COVID-19. He already had a trach, so putting him on a ventilator was quite simple and the obvious next step.

At some point after arriving at the hospital, I sent out a mass text to our families and my pastor. Time seemed to be both flying by and standing still all at once. I didn't feel like I had a second to spare in getting to the hospital to inform them beforehand. Our parents and Pastor Jeff immediately went into prayer mode and sent out prayer requests to everyone they could think of. My mom and sister were standing by, ready to come to me when summoned.

I communicated with the staff through my grief and worry-strained throat, having once again to function with a cannonball-sized hole through my gut. I did what I could from the doorway to get Sam to respond. He looked pink and sweaty, but his eyes looked good—clear. He looked alert and peaceful, but he couldn't follow any commands. I asked him to wave to me, give me a thumbs-up, anything. No response. He just looked at me calmly with his beautiful teal-blue eyes, always set off by the blue and green hospital gown.

He was sliding further downhill, and they decided to take him to the ICU immediately. Even in the thirty-or-so yards between the ER and ICU, he was going south. They put me in the familiar ICU waiting room. Within a few minutes, the words I dreaded most came over the overhead speaker, "Code blue ICU B," followed by familiar staff members running down the hallway. My body turned to ice.

We'd had more close calls than I can count, but this was different. I tried to be hopeful, but I'd never felt this before. I prayed. After another few minutes, a nurse I knew from the second-floor telemetry unit came to sit with me. She just happened to be in the ICU, and when she saw it was Sam who coded, she came to find me and be with me. I knew from her presence that this was it.

My mom and sister were now on their way, and the security guard—who happened to be an old ROTC friend and Army vet—was told to let them in. I still had a glimmer of hope; Sam had beaten the odds so many times before. Another nurse came in, probably followed by a doctor, but it's all a grief-fogged blur. That was it. They did the best they could.

It was about seven hours from when Sam spiked a fever until his heart stopped. Almost thirteen years after he survived the IED that took the lives of four good men, he joined them in Valhalla.

My nurse friend sat with me until and even after my mom arrived. My sister arrived shortly after, and she thankfully volunteered to call Donny. "Donny…," she choked out, "he's gone." She asked him to pass the word to their parents and brother Marty. I'm doing my best to remember, but much of this is a frozen blur. Frozen in pain, in disbelief, in grief.

You don't want to be well-known at the hospital, but it can be a scary and lonely place. Friendly, comforting faces and a shoulder to cry on when I needed it was a tremendous blessing. I'm so glad that when Sam passed, we had staff who knew us well to help us. We couldn't have asked for better care. I say "we" because, although Sam was the patient, they cared for me as well—right up to the very end.

# AFTER

Grief is a funny thing. Not funny, ha-ha, but, you know… mysterious, or something. It's both universal and completely individual. To be human and in relationship with other beings means you will experience grief many times over, yet we all experience it uniquely. Even your own family's experiences with grief can vary widely from each other.

Because grief is both universal and individual, it's easy to project our own feelings onto others, and that may look like judgment. To someone looking on, my inability to feel all but the most tragic of circumstances may come off as cold, to another, tough, to some, sad. I even judged my own initial grief when Sam passed.

When I heard "Code blue ICU B" over the intercom, my body went ice cold. By the time he was gone, I was numb. First frozen, then numb from the fear and the grief. Tears came on their own, but I was remarkably calm. No sob caught in my chest. Even in that moment, I was judging my own grief, my lack of reaction.

When my mom arrived and heard the news, she had the dramatic, sobbing, and wailing reaction that I would have expected from myself. If I loved him like I knew I did, shouldn't I be reacting like her? I just observed her outward show of grief while my inward pain concentrated in my solar plexus, a black hole pulling all my nerve endings into my core and depriving the rest of my body of feeling.

Still, I wondered, shouldn't I be a huddled mass on the floor? Isn't that what people do? It's what I expected I would do the countless times I had waking nightmares of the end. I pictured throwing myself on his body– my body wracked with uncontrollable, gut-wrenching sobs, unable to tear myself away from the final goodbye. In reality, it was nothing like that.

I was brought back to the eerily quiet ICU, in a familiar special isolation room where he'd previously been a resident. It was darker than I remembered, but it was after 11:00 p.m. by then, so the lights would have been low to let patients sleep.

This was the moment I'd been dreading since the day Sam stepped on the boot camp yellow footprints in San Diego.

As was the case numerous times before, because of all his superbugs, I had to touch my husband through nitrile gloves, wearing a yellow isolation gown and mask. I'd been training for this for seventeen years. In the dimly lit silence of this ICU isolation room, I touched him, stared at him, and took him in. I laid my chest on his, buried my head in the nook under his chin, and put his limp arm around me for one last time, the weight a comfort.

I don't think I stayed long. I got what I needed. He was dead. There was nothing more I could do. There was no doctor to strategize with or nurses and therapists to plan with. It was just over. Sam was gone, and I had to step away. I'd walked out of that ICU countless times before, but I always expected to be back.

Did I do it right?

I know there is no right way to grieve. And I hate that I sullied mourning Sam with judgment about why I was reacting the way I did. That I even had the thought instead of being fully present in the moment still hurts me. I feel sorry about judging myself for the way I grieved.

My numbness continued for well over a year, thawing and becoming raw at times but returning to the safety of numbness. Providentially, I started therapy for anxiety and depression three weeks before Sam died, so I had immediate help.

My therapist encouraged me to talk about my feelings. I didn't know what they were, though. I can't identify what I can't feel. The numbness was so intense I literally googled, "what do emotions feel like?"

In the first several days, probably weeks, after Sam died, I lived in my spot on the couch. My mom came to stay with me immediately, and my dad, sister, and her kids were often home with me.

The tears fell and fell. Sometimes, there was a trigger, like a kind text, a card, or a care package delivery (thanks for the hard seltzer, Betty). But often, they just came of their own accord, seemingly from nowhere.

I rarely sobbed. I was too numb to feel the depth of emotion that conjures a sob. It was more like a systemic sadness had infiltrated every cell in my body. I was both depressed and anxious, unable to unclench my abs or keep my eyes dry.

# CHAPTER SEVENTEEN

# GOODBYE, SAM

People tried to comfort me with platitudes about Sam no longer being in pain or in a broken, sick body. The thing is, he wasn't in pain. He never complained of pain other than the occasional headache. For those who weren't with him, who didn't see how much life he had, I can see how the severity of his disability would be hard to get past. For me, though, I knew how great a life he had right up to the very end.

He never complained of pain and only rarely acknowledged he had any deficits, a blessing of having a right hemisphere brain injury. When our pastor, Jeff, came for his weekly visits, Sam's prayer requests were always about me—my safety, my health, my happiness. One time, though, his prayer request was that God would take the fog from his mind. That was the only time I ever heard him mention his own cognitive state.

I wasn't relieved when he passed. It's really hard for people to understand how a person so severely disabled could lead a good life because we can't imagine how something so far from the norm can be someone's normal. Sam wasn't old, frail, or miserable. Despite his deficits and his medically fragile state, he was happy and had a good quality of life. There was no misery from which to be relieved. I'm only sad and heartbroken that my best friend is gone. I miss him every day.

## ANGER

I get asked a lot about anger. Am I angry that Sam died of COVID? Am I angry that I couldn't be with him in person for the last three weeks of his life or that I couldn't even touch skin-to-skin with my just-deceased husband? Actually...no.

I admit that I still have a hard time feeling and identifying emotions (just ask my therapist), but I honestly don't believe I am or ever have been angry about anything that happened to Sam. It sucks. It sucks hard, but I don't see a reason to be angry about it.

And maybe I have a flawed idea about what anger even means. To me, anger connotes blame and wrongdoing. If someone causes an accident due to reckless or irresponsible behavior, if you wrong one of my people, I'm pissed, and I turn into a mama bear.

When it's a shitty situation not caused by anyone in particular, I'm not mad. If you're angry, it begs the question, angry at whom? God? I'm not mad at God. I don't understand His ways, but I do firmly believe Romans 8:28, which states, "And we know that for those who love God all things work together for good for those who are called according to his purpose." It's a hard truth, but as a Christian, this is what I believe. I believe it to my core, and I believe this truth, in particular, is what has gotten me through every day since I was saved just weeks after Sam's injury.

So, I'm not angry, and I know that surprises many people, but it surprises me to know how many people are angry. As I work in therapy on breaking down the defensive walls I've built to protect myself, anger is not an emotion I feel I need to be more in touch with. What good does it serve? Like the "angry wife" from the conference in Texas, from my perspective, anger just brings misery.

So, what about the stages of grief? The five stages of grief as we know them are a framework developed by Elizabeth Kubler Ross to identify and help navigate loss. They can be helpful, but they're not prescriptive. Their ubiquitousness in our understanding of grief and loss has clouded my own perception of how to grieve, even to secretly believe that grief should look a certain way.

I don't believe I experienced most of the Kubler-Ross stages of grief: denial, anger, bargaining, depression, and acceptance. There was undoubtedly a sense of "I can't believe this is really happening," but I was never in denial of Sam's death. I prayed while he was dying, but I didn't promise God I'd be a good girl if He let Sam live, and I definitely didn't experience anger.

Depression? Now we're talking. Then again, I'd just received a diagnosis of major clinical depression weeks before Sam died, so that was an easy one. Even acceptance is far easier for me than anger. Both when Sam was first injured and when he ultimately died, I think I moved into acceptance pretty quickly.

My ability to get to acceptance may be part of my "control the controllable" attitude toward life. We can't control the fact that shit happens, but we can control our response to the shit. It sounds calculated, but this comes naturally to me, and as hard as it may be for people to understand, anger just doesn't, and I'm happy with that. I think Sam would be, too.

## QUESTIONING

Who am I without Sam? I have been Sam's for more of my life than I have not been. In high school, I thought of us as "SamnErin," one word like the twins, "Samnerik" from Lord of the Flies.

I experienced some existential crises about who I am without Sam during boot camp and his deployments, but I was still *his* during these times. I remember watching one of the first few seasons of American Idol with my mother-in-law, thinking I'd never watch this if Sam were here, but I'm kind of into it. I realized that on my own, I'd rather watch Gilmore Girls than South Park. I had my own tastes, and it was alright that they were starkly different from Sam's. In fact, my weekly Gilmore Girls viewing turned into Sam's weekly quiet reading session. I'd watch "my show" in the living room, and he'd retreat to the bedroom with a book.

These individualities of mine took time to surface. Sam's interests had shaped my taste in everything from music to movies to TV. My identity was always wrapped in my relationship with him. That's only just begun to change. I will always be Sam's widow now, but my sense of self is finally detaching from him.

For well over a year after his death, I felt a kind of victimhood. I was in a very passive and reactionary state—the state of having become a widow. Everything from the box I check on official documents to how I spend my days had changed.

Not only my husband and best friend but my way of life was taken away. I no longer spend the middle six or so hours of my day in Granite Bay at Care Meridian with Sam. Even my gym changed. It doesn't make sense anymore to belong to the gym five minutes from him but twelve minutes from home.

Who am I without Sam? Who are any of us when we are no longer associated with a core piece of our life? I imagine empty nesters and the recently retired have a similar feeling.

My daily life and routines have become my new normal, just as we adjusted to life post-injury. Finding that new rhythm was a huge adjustment not made any easier by dealing with my newly diagnosed depression, anxiety, and ADHD, along with my ever-lingering and evolving grief. I still deal with all those things, but I'm living my new normal. The books I read, the music I listen to, and the TV and movies I watch aren't influenced by Sam, but I still struggle with the question of who Erin is. I was very comfortable with "SamnErin," or even Sam and Erin, but Erin, solo, is still new to me.

## MY POST-MORTEM

The last two-plus years have felt like both an eternity and like time flew by during the tornado in Oklahoma. Days seem to crawl by, especially the bad ones, but the weeks vanish one after the next, and I can't believe Sam's been gone for so long. I have new routines, and despite once feeling like life without Sam could never feel normal, I have my new normal.

I work as an online health coach out of a co-working space in Historic Folsom, where I also train a few people in person. I recently began training at my gym, just a few minutes from my house, and I love the variety and structure it added to my days.

My morning routine is hugely important to me, as I think it should be for everyone. I believe, especially when you spend your day taking care of other people and hearing about their struggles, it's essential to start the day with time just for you. I'd rather wake up early and have a leisurely morning doing things important to me than sleep later and be instantly in get-up-and-go mode.

My day starts at 5:00 a.m., and I immediately make my bed and then head for the coffee. If I was on top of things the night before, it's already made, programmed to start at 4:50 a.m. But first… water. As I pour my first cup of coffee, I also make sure my water bottle is full and drink ten glugs of water before I get my first coffee sip.

Hydrated with coffee at my side, I start the day with prayer and reading a chapter or two in my Bible, followed by gratitude and affirmations in my journal, and then I read non-fiction for the remainder of the 5:00 hour. At 6:00 a.m., I'm either off to train at the gym or switch my reading to fiction until it's time to get ready for the day. Carving out time for these important-to-me activities gives me the structure I need to start my day off well.

My weekdays vary from day to day based on clients, but Wednesdays are always for the kids. My brother-in-law drops off my nieces and nephew around 7:00 a.m., and they're mine until about 4:00 p.m. Holly (13) and Sam (10—named after Uncle Sam) go to school just five minutes from my house, and little Charlotte (4—or Charlie, as we call her) stays home to play with me.

As much as my life has changed since Sam died, having the kids on Wednesdays has been a constant. Since Holly was about five months old, I've been blessed to be at least a weekly part of their lives. I'll likely never have my own kids. Sam and I wanted to wait until after he was out of the Marine Corps and we were closer to thirty to start a family. I'm more than happy being "Tee-Tee" now.

The first week or so after Sam died, my sister was over with the kids a lot. They were amazing. As much as I wanted to be strong in front of them, worried I'd scare them, they were incredible and brought light and hope into an otherwise very dark time. Uncle Sam had been a big part of their lives, and it was a loss for them as well. They were, of course, also dealing with living through the beginning of the pandemic, missing their friends, and figuring out virtual school.

Charlie asks about the pictures of Uncle Sam, even pictures of herself in his lap. Holly and Sam, though, grew up visiting and playing with Uncle Sam. I hope their experience with him and the other patients at Care Meridian will shape their empathy and compassion for others.

As much of a salve to my pain as the kids are, grief and mental health have been a battle. I'd started therapy in March 2020, just before the shutdown and before Sam died. Post-shut down, the second session with my therapist was virtual, and I had a heartbreaking answer to the question of how's it going.

Much of the last two years have been spent dealing with grief, which muddies the waters around my other issues regarding depression, anxiety, trauma, avoidance, and attention. I went from being afraid to admit to myself that I have any mental health struggles to being buried in a suffocating dog pile of diagnoses and symptoms. Is it really depression if it's grief? Am I still grieving the injury from 2007 that I never really dealt with? How much does trauma affect all of this? Do I actually have ADHD, or is it just a symptom of trauma or anxiety? We're still working these things out.

I have good days and bad days, and am so far still struggling with depression. It started with the second anniversary of Sam's death on April 3. The first anniversary went smoothly. I went to a baseball game with my cousin, Callie, and did my best compartmentalizing job yet. I knew what day it was, yet was able to focus on the present and have a good time.

This year was different. I was in Nashville for business on the anniversary with my business coaches and our family of coaches at a fabulous Airbnb for the morning. Then, I went with the wife of a Marine Corps buddy to surprise her husband at a local BBQ joint.

It was a great day until I was alone at my hotel. As soon as my friends dropped me off at my hotel, I got a killer headache, took some Tylenol, and laid down for a while. But I just couldn't get comfortable, and not wanting to waste the afternoon, I took an Uber to a local bookstore in a trendy area of Nashville. I love buying a book at an independent bookstore whenever I travel.

I planned to pick up some water and a couple of protein bars and snacks at the Kroger's down the street when I noticed TailGate Brewery, a place I'd been to with a friend on another Nashville visit. An early pizza and beer dinner was exactly what I needed—I even had a couple of new books to keep me company.

Beer in hand, waiting for my pizza, the feelings started washing over me. There was no conscious thought, just a tidal wave of emotion and grief that hit me like a double shot on an empty stomach. I rushed into the bathroom. All I could afford was a small cry, and I certainly couldn't release the emotional kraken raging inside me—I still had to go back into the restaurant and get myself back to my hotel. Splashing my face with cold water helped pull me together.

My throat was tight, and tears kept threatening to escape all through eating my pizza, drinking my beer, and reading *Winter in Sokcho* by Elisa Shua Dusapin. But I made it until I got back to my hotel and could let go. I felt so alone. I felt so uncomfortable in my skin and in my situation. I wanted to be with someone but also needed to be alone. I could have called someone, but I didn't know what to say. I didn't feel like anyone could actually help. I figured it was important, so I stayed with my sadness and felt what I was feeling. It was one of my deepest, darkest moments of grief.

I've had a lot of bad days since then, but what brings about a bad day usually seems arbitrary. Like the other day, it was terrible. I was an emotional dumpster fire, probably because the day before had been Sam's birthday, and the previous Saturday, his grandpa, Earl, passed away. I felt like I'd never feel any better, like I hadn't made any progress in over two years of grieving, and like I just didn't know what to do with myself. I had a hard but good therapy session, and the next day was absolutely fine.

Bad days seem to hit like a tornado. Some days hit me square in the face with the funnel cloud, while most skate by with only minimal damage. Some days, there isn't a cloud in the sky.

As difficult as the hard times are, I've come a long way in the past two-plus years. Honestly, just being able to talk about and write about my feelings is a huge improvement. Deployment mode is over. You don't have to protect a broken heart, but you can do your best to put it back together.

# CHAPTER EIGHTEEN

# MY EPILOGUE

I recently read a book where the main character becomes a widow. I read it through tears. I will never not be a widow, so my worldview will always be tinted, seen through a widow's black veil. She was on the moon when her husband was killed on Earth and so had no way of being with him. I don't know if I was so touched by this fictional turn of events because it was just sad or because I relate to the main character as a fellow widow with striking similarities—kept from her husband in his final weeks and had to plan an unconventional memorial service months after his death. Some books, mostly fiction, have an ending followed by an epilogue. Movies do this, too. In particular, I'm thinking of The Sandlot. The epilogue gives us a sense of what the characters are doing in the future.

Looking to a future without Sam is still foreign to me. For my entire adult life, save the last two years, my future depended on Sam–Sam's orders, Sam's safety, Sam's recovery, Sam's health, Sam's survival. I still find it hard to dream and plan for my future. My dreams at night still include Sam. While I don't know exactly what my future holds, what I do know is that despite my struggles–emotional, mental, or otherwise—I still have choices, and the promise I made to Sam twenty years ago is my epilogue.

Months after I finished writing this book, I had an epiphany. It all started at Olive Garden. I had a gift card left over from a care package given to me after Sam died, so I decided to take myself out. Sitting alone with a glass of wine and a book (the trusty companion of the unaccompanied), waiting for my pasta dinner to arrive, it hit me: If I can go out to eat alone, I can go to Hawaii alone.

Hawaii was on my mind after a conversation with friends a few days earlier during a sixty-five-mile relay race from San Francisco to Penngrove. Sitting in the shade on the side of the road in Petaluma, waiting for Stephanie to finish her ten-mile leg and pass the baton off to me to finish our race, Marssie asked our relay team if we could live anywhere in the world, money and life circumstances irrelevant, where would it be. Without hesitation, Annie answered Maui.

I'd never been to Hawaii, and this conversation planted a seed. Sitting there at Olive Garden, I decided to go for it. I was going to Hawaii… alone. I planned the trip for just after my thirty-ninth birthday.

The first week of December, I spent at Ka'anapli Shores on Maui and traveled all over the island. I snorkeled, swam with a turtle, hiked, swam under waterfalls, read for hours on the beach, and even met up with some friends and friends of friends. It was the perfect combination of solitude and socializing, adventure, and rest.

Sacramento was dreary and rainy when I returned from paradise. Within a few days, I was broadsided by depression, back in the funk I was always trying to avoid and doing the bare minimum, just surviving each day. I showed up to work and did my best to serve my clients well, but if I didn't have to be somewhere, I was likely taking a nap on the couch, sleeping at all hours of the day.

About a week into my funk, I had a Zoom meeting in preparation for TedX Folsom. Jen was in charge of the volunteers, and we were touching base on plans for the upcoming event. Rather than asking me what most people asked: "What was your favorite part?" Jen asked the question that changed my life.

"What did you learn about yourself on your trip?" My initial response was that I thrive spending time outside. I'd just come from eighty-degree paradise, spending most of my waking hours basking in the sun, gazing at the ocean, waterfalls, and jungle, to six weeks of relentless rain and cold–cold for California anyway. It added up. Sunny outdoor Erin equals thriving. Cold and wet Erin equals barely hanging on.

Right then, I committed to myself, and Jen for accountability, to get outside every day for at least a short walk, even if it was in the rain. It helped. I began to slowly crawl out of my depressive funk and feel more and more like myself.

That wasn't the answer, though. Jen's question kept plaguing me. During the week between Christmas and New Year's, on a walk during a break in the rain, I meditated on the question. What did I learn about myself? Sadly, I can't control the weather, and moving to Maui isn't an option. So, what was different about the way I approached life on Maui compared to my everyday life?

Obviously, I didn't have the obligations and responsibilities of normal life on Maui, but it was more than that. I only had seven days on Maui. Each day, my mission was to answer: how could I make this the best day possible? I was actively seeking to thrive each day—to live as an action verb.

Having two service-based jobs, my daily schedule varies. One Monday isn't going to look like the next Monday and each day of the week has its own flavor. I'd look at my calendar for the week and schedule for the day, looking not for what the day entailed but for when I would be done with work. What time did I get to start enjoying myself? As much as I love what I do, I looked at my calendar with disdain rather than delight. I was stifling myself, and setting up each day as something I had to get through.

Who knows the next time I'll get to spend a week in paradise? What kind of life am I living if I'm just trying to get through my day until I get to some special event I'm actually looking forward to? That's not living; that's simply existing.

How could I take my Maui mentality into my daily life? I've always loved the expression, "It's a great day for a great day." That's it! It's a great day for a great day–ALL day. It was time to live it.

This is how I've approached life ever since. It's a great day for a great day–ALL day. Whether I'm on coaching calls, in meetings, training clients at the gym, or hanging out with my friends, I can enjoy myself. It's a choice. I don't have to wait until I have free time to have a good time.

This paradigm shift has made a tremendous difference in how I show up for myself and, likewise, how I show up for the people I serve in my life, whether it be my family and friends or my clients.

I genuinely now look at my day as an opportunity rather than a slog. I get to train and coach "x" number of clients today, and that's awesome. I'm done working whenever I'm done working for the day, but I don't have to wait to be happy.

I get to choose to be happy right now.

I get to choose to carry on.

I get to choose gratitude.

I get to choose to show up and try my damnedest to be the best version of myself each and every day. And I get to choose to keep fulfilling the promise Sam and I made to each other twenty years ago:

I will never let myself go. I will never stop striving to better myself, to challenge what is possible, to choose happiness—no matter what.

## CONVERSATIONS WITH SAM

Following are some special conversations I had with Sam after his injury that will always make me smile.

Sam Nichols had a great communication day, and I like to take advantage of those. I posed a scenario to him. I asked him to imagine it was five years after he died, and his family and friends got together to celebrate his memory over some beers. What would he want them to remember about him? Finish the sentence: Sam was…

His answer: Sam was fair, a good leader, a great fighter, excitable, heroic, always had good beer, was a helluva good dancer, and was unimaginably sweet.

## BLOODWORK

Erin: The guy from the lab is here to take your blood.

Sam: Do you know why they want my blood? I do.

Erin: Tell me.

Sam: They want to clone me.

Erin: Oh. I can see why they'd want to, but why clone you?

Sam: They wanna clone me because I'm a great swordsman.

Erin: You are. Who wants to clone you?

Sam: The Foot Clan.

Erin: Tell me about them.

Sam: They're gangsters. Japanese gangsters.

Erin: Wow. They might want to clone you, but the guy here today is just checking your ptINR, which has to do with the thickness or thinness of your blood. It's important for a swordsman's blood not to be too thin.

Sam: You got that right.

I later figured out the Foot Clan is from Teenage Mutant Ninja Turtles.

## COUPLE

Sam: Erin

Erin: Yeah?

Sam: Can we be a couple?

Erin: You mean like boyfriend and girlfriend?

Sam: Yeah

Erin: I would love that.

Sam: I would love that too.

## HAIRCUT

Sam: You never commented on my hair.

Erin: I'm sorry, was I supposed to?

Sam: I got it cut.

Erin: I know. I'm your barber.

Sam: Oh. Good work.

## INTEGRITY

Sam and I were hanging out in his room watching TV.

Sam: I have to quit working here.

Erin: Why?

Sam: They are just too dishonest.

Erin: What kind of place is this?

Sam: Bowling alley.

Erin: I want to know more about this.

Sam: They're criminals.

Erin: Like, how? What are they doing?

Sam: Everything. It's a crime ring.

Erin: So is the bowling alley just a front?

Sam: Yep.

Erin: They're not trying to get you involved, are they?

Sam: No. I keep my nose clean.

Erin: So how do you know about it?

Sam: I just know.

## THANKSGIVING

Erin: Tomorrow is Thanksgiving. What are you thankful for?

Sam: I'm thankful for all my family does to put it all together.

Erin: All the food?

Sam: No. Just life.

Erin: Awww. That's nice.

Sam: And my friends.

Erin: Which category do I fit into?

Sam: Friend.

Erin: I thought maybe I'd be both. Do you remember that we're married?

Sam: No. We're not married.

Erin: Well, do you think one day we will be?

Sam: Yeah.

Erin: I wanna be in both categories. What are my chances?

Sam: Wondrous.

## TOO YOUNG FOR LOVE?

Erin: I love you.

Sam: I love you too, but you're too young to know what love is.

Erin: I'm older than you.

Sam: I know that.

Erin: So, we're too young for love?

Sam: Maybe we are.

Erin: How old do you have to be to know if you're really in love?

Sam: 25-ish.

Erin: And how old are we?

Sam: 20-ish (actually, 35 and 36).

Erin: So are we the exception?

Sam: We must be.

## GET MARRIED

Sam: Wanna get married?

Erin: Yeah, but why do you want to marry me?

Sam: I just do.

Erin: What if I told you we've been married for a long time? We got married a couple months before boot camp.

Sam: I'm not being paid for being married.

Erin: You get paid for having a dependent.

Sam: I need to call someone about my account.

Erin: It's all taken care of. Don't worry about it.

Sam: I need to make sure they have my correct information.

## LITTLE DARLING

Erin: I love you.

Sam: I love you, my little darling.

Erin: That's a new thing you've been calling me–little darling.

Sam: You're just so cute.

## MAGIC TRICK

Sam: Hey guys. Wanna see a magic trick?

Nurse and I: Yeah!

Sam: Proceeds to raise his hand to cover his face and make a host of facial expressions, especially with his eyebrows.

(Not sure what he actually intended, but it was a good show).

## 36?

Sam: You're 36?

Erin: I will be in a couple weeks.

Sam: No, I'm being realistic.

Erin: You mean you wanna know my real age?

Sam: Please.

Erin: I am 35, and I'll be 36 in about two weeks.

Sam: How is that possible?

Erin explains the time frame of his injury and reminds him of his TBI and short-term memory loss.

Erin: You know what's cool about us being 35?

Sam: What?

Erin: It means we've been married 16 years.

Sam: That's how old I am now.

## BESTIE

While listening to a podcast, Sam learned the term "bestie".

He said "that's a funny word." He likes it though.

## I LOVE IT

A very sleepy Sam Nichols says, "Thank you for being right here to love. I love it."

## ANNIVERSARY

Erin: Thank you for all the anniversary love.

Sam: What are we supposed to be doing today?

Me: Enjoying each other.

Sam: I'm enjoying you very much.

## 15TH ANNIVERSARY

Erin: Today's our anniversary!

Sam: I can't believe it's been a year already.

## I THINK HE LIKES ME

So far today, Sam has hit on me because he thought it was before we were together. He asked me when Valentine's Day was, and he asked me what's happening this month (our anniversary is in two days). I think he likes me. He also pointed out that we're "kinda wearing the same thing." We're both in athletic black bottoms, green shirts, and running shoes.

## FIVE MORE MINUTES

Sam and I were cuddling in bed.

Sam: Just five more minutes. Then you can do your chores.

## LOVE AT FIRST SIGHT

I just got to Sam's.

Sam: I've thought about you ever since I first saw you.

## LOOKING

I'm standing in Sam's room while he lies in bed.

Erin: Do you have an itch? Are you stretching?

Sam: I'm looking for you.

Erin: Here I am.(I go over and give him a hug and kiss, taking a picture as I do).

Sam: How'd it turn out? I feel like I looked goofy.

## AGE

Sam keeps asking me what year it is and how old we are. He keeps saying, "But you haven't aged a day." He's the best husband without even trying.

## VOTE FOR ME

Sam just randomly asked me if I would vote for him for student council president.

Sam: Do you have a camera?

Erin: Yeah. Why?

Sam: Take my campaign photo.

Sam proceeds to flex his right arm and grin his lopsided grin.

## THERAPY

After orienting Sam…

Erin: Do you have any questions?

Sam: Yeah, when is my Erin therapy?


## WAITING ROOM

Sam and I are waiting to be seen at the VA.

Erin: Look, they have Highlights!

Sam: I gotta read that!


## FACETIMING DURING COVID-19 ISOLATION

Sam's SLP was helping him speak loudly and have a conversation with me. She prompted him to tell me he missed me. What Sam actually said was, "I wanna take your pants off."

# ACKNOWLEDGMENTS

This book came to be via countless requests from the horde of people who followed our story through social media for thirteen unrelenting years. Through your prayers and support, I didn't feel alone. I had a team of thousands praying and cheering us on through endless infections and hospitalizations, as well as the many victories we celebrated through Sam's recovery and rehabilitation. Thank you for being there.

I can't go another sentence without thanking all of the medical personnel who worked tirelessly to keep Sam alive and progressing for nearly thirteen years after that fateful day in 2007. To our Corpsmen in the field, Doc Patrick Couhie and Doc James Hansen, the medevac and medical team in Baghdad, our medical teams in Landstuhl and Bethesda, and our Air Force medevac crews who brought us back home, I can't thank you enough for giving Sam a chance at life. To the unknown individuals who played a part in saving Sam's life, including those who provided their own blood for transfusions in Baghdad, I thank you with my whole heart.

Sam received incredible care from the team at the Palo Alto VA, Kentfield Rehabilitation Hospital, especially Dr. Doherty, Dr. Waters, Dr. Duncan, and Chaplain Betsy Rosen. I am eternally grateful for your care of Sam and what you taught me. Our nurses, nursing assistants (CNAs), and therapists became my friends and support system when I was alone day after day. You not only took great care of Sam, but you provided me with the companionship and levity I needed at such a vulnerable and painful time.

Our hometown medical team at Care Meridian became family and they treated Sam like a son and brother. I especially want to thank our nurses—Annie, Hira, and Jhanek, and our therapy team Sue, Kari, Eileen, Roz, Cheryl, and Celeste. You always believed in Sam, and you were like big sisters to me. I'm actually crying as I type this. I love you. Poppy, our "house mom," you were such a beacon of love and light. To our CNAs, you dealt with both the grumpiest and charming versions of Sam. You worked so lovingly to make sure he was clean, safe, comfortable, and entertained. I love you.

It's never a result of pleasant circumstances to be well known at a hospital, but it's more comforting than I can put into words to have nurses, respiratory therapists, CNAs, security guards, chaplains, and doctors who all know you well. To our staff at Sutter Roseville Hospital, I am beyond grateful for your care of not only Sam, but of me. For nearly eleven years you did everything you could to give Sam another chance at life, and you gave me hope time and time again.

To our Kilo 3/12 (Sam's unit) family, I love you. Whether it be through phone calls and texts, Facebook messages, fundraising, or trips to come out and see us, you truly demonstrated—and continue to demonstrate—brotherly love. You embody Semper Fidelis. Sam loved hearing about you guys and his whole demeanor changed when you came to visit. When you were with him, I saw Sam the proud, broad-shouldered marine instead of Sam the TBI patient. You were stalwart brothers to Sam, and you continue to be my brothers. Frater Infinitas.

Sam and I were blessed with a loving and supportive family. To Sam's parents, Eric and Kelley, who love me like their own daughter—I especially appreciate your allowing me to make the decisions regarding Sam's care and supporting those decisions no matter what. You never fought me, and only ever encouraged me. To your spouses, Wendy and Jose, you loved and prayed for Sam as if he were your own flesh and blood, and you continue to love me the same. To my parents, Julie and Tony, you have always loved me unconditionally, and took Sam in as your own son. My loss and grief was your loss and grief, and I couldn't have asked for anything more from you.

To our siblings, Marty, Donny, and Brandi, and to Ali and Luis, you are the friends I needed through the toughest times. Donny, you endured the grueling and emotional travel with me in the first days, and took care of me like the big brother you are. I know you were suffering too, but you took care of me—trying to get food in me, being my shoulder to cry on, and especially keeping me sane with your dark humor. Brandi, you became my sister when I needed all the sisters I could get. I will forever think of you when I see MadLibs. Marty, I know you love deeply, and Sam's injury hurt you to your core. We love you. Ali, you loved Sam like your flesh and blood brother, as he loved and protected you. You've been there for me from the start, even though you were so young when the injury happened—you stepped up as only a sister can. I can't thank you enough for bringing your children into the world and sharing them with us. Uncle Sam loved them, and he was always so touched that you named your son after him every time I reminded him. Our time at Care Meridian is dotted with memories of the kids growing up and playing with Uncle Sam and his toys. Luis, I'm so sad you never got to know Sam before his injury. I am confident you two would have been best friends. I am blessed to have you as my friend and brother.

Sixteen years have passed since Sam's injury, and through those years I've collected friends along the way who helped me through those years of uncertainty and pain, infection after infection, hospitalization after hospitalization. Whether it was hours of companionship and therapy on long bike rides or runs, or love and support through social media and text, I thank my "endurance" friends. You allowed me time to be free, to challenge myself physically, and to recharge when I so desperately needed it. Special thanks to Elyse, Lindsay, Stacey, Betty, and Suzanne. You listened, visited, cooked for me, stocked my fridge, and were there in any way I needed you, and I did need you. Suzanne and Raul, you are the big sister and brother I needed. I know I can always turn to you.

I don't mention my time in college and grad school much in the book, but the friends I made at Sac State were invaluable. Wyme, Tammy, Kasie, Petra, Geneva, and Megan, you saw the worst of me at times and helped me grow up to become a better friend. You listened to me and endured my self-centeredness—I wouldn't have made it through school without you.

My church family has been a huge support for me. I know I can count on any of you. Jeff and Dan visited Sam and me every week, providing needed male companionship and discipleship. Linda, your daily scripture, which I often read aloud to Sam, never goes unappreciated. My book club girls are so supportive and have been cheering me on in this project from the beginning. I especially appreciate your Christian friendship.

To my Granite City Coworking family, you are an inspiration to me and have helped me level up. Annie, I love you. Your belief in me and constant cheerleading have pulled me through some tough days.

Natasha, thank you for your excitement and belief in this book, and for introducing me to Kelley.

To Kelley, my writing coach and publisher, thank you for getting me across the finish line. I know I did the work, but I couldn't have brought it to fruition without you. Thank you for dealing with my salty snark, pulling the emotion out of me when I was still defrosting, and pushing me to finish. I'm honored to write the first memoir published by Redcliff, and you know the name has a special meaning to me.

After I finished the second draft, I asked for volunteers to read it through and provide their honest feedback. Thank you so much to the brave souls who not only read that early version but provided thoughtful notes. You made me dig deeper and explore areas I hadn't considered. Thank you for helping me make this story more complete and more authentic.

I can't finish without thanking my English teachers who taught and encouraged me at different stages of my development. Mrs. Clark, you gave me a love of English and made me believe for the first time that I was good at something academic. Mrs. Kozumplik and Ms. Cameron, aside from teaching me, you encouraged me to write by bolstering my confidence. Finally, Leslie Cooper, you pushed me like no other teacher ever did, and I am better for it. You were the first to read the very first stories of this book. Your reassurance and excitement over my early draft emboldened my resolve to continue on.

When I first conceived of this book at 3:00 am in 2019, I never truly imagined it being a physical book in print, but here we are. Everyone mentioned above, and so many I haven't mentioned, including the thousands of anonymous people who prayed for Sam, are part of making this book and memorial to our great love a reality. With all my heart, I thank you.

# ABOUT THE AUTHOR

Erin Nichols grew up and still resides in the Sacramento area of Northern California. She loves nature, spending time outdoors, reading, and always looks forward to her next adventure. She graduated from California State University, Sacramento with a master's in Speech-Language Pathology. Erin works as a personal trainer and nutrition coach to help others push past the boundaries of their comfort zone and realize their full potential.

Printed in the USA
CPSIA information can be obtained
at www.ICGtesting.com
LVHW051028241223
767334LV00012B/1012